IDEA®
Picture
Dictionary

An IDEA® Language Development Resource

BALLARD & TIGHE
PUBLISHERS

Brea, California

Phonics Consultant

Dr. Norma Inabinette received her doctorate in education and psychology from the University of Buffalo. She is a professor emeritus at California State University, Fullerton. Her 27-year teaching career included a specialization in the diagnosis of reading disabilities and remedial instruction. She also directed the campus reading clinic, providing instruction to community members with reading disabilities. She currently conducts staff development and consults with school districts, publishers, and community agencies throughout Southern California.

Language Development Consultant

Bonnie McKenna received her teaching credential from the University of California, Riverside and her TESL certificate and CLAD credential from the University of California, Irvine. She has been an educator for more than thirty years, working as an elementary-level teacher, a college lecturer, and a teacher of adult ESL. She currently teaches and develops curriculum for the Community Based English Tutoring (CBET) program in the Capistrano Unified School District in California. She was one of the first teachers to pioneer the CBET program in 1999.

Reviewers

The *IDEA Picture Dictionary* greatly benefited from the educators who carefully reviewed the dictionary and provided helpful comments and suggestions.

> Patricia Amaya-Thetford, Alcott Elementary School, Pomona, California
> Gilda Bazan-Lopez, Educational Consultant, Houston, Texas
> Beverly Crowe, Gallup-McKinley County Public Schools, Gallup, New Mexico
> Gretchen Gross, Yuma District #1, Yuma, Arizona
> Dr. Joyce Lancaster, Educational Consultant, Tampa, Florida
> Robyn Ospital, La Habra City School District, La Habra, California
> Dr. Betsy Rymes, University of Georgia, Athens, Georgia
> Dr. Patricia Sanchez-Diaz, Parent Consultant, Menlo Park, California
> Karen Shaw, Educational Consultant, Brea, California
> Caryn Sonberg, Cora Kelly Magnet School, Alexandria, Virginia
> Ann Stekelberg, Majestic Way Elementary School, San Jose, California
> Dr. Connie Williams, Educational Consultant, Menlo Park, California

Translators

Providing the *IDEA Picture Dictionary* words in six different languages would not have been possible without the talents and dedication of the following translators: Bob Batson, David Brisco, David Goetz, George Hsieh, Chue Lao, Leonor Morris, Cathy Sanchez, and Omega Translation Service.

An IDEA® Language Development Resource

Managing Editor: Laurie Regan
Editor: Dr. Roberta Stathis
Editorial Staff: Kristin Belsher, Veronica Jauriqui, and Allison Mangrum
Program Consultants: Virginia Andrade, David Brisco, and Patrice Sonberg Gotsch
Desktop Publishing Coordinator: Kathleen Styffe
Graphic Designers: George Hsieh, Joseph Montoya, and Charles W. Shaffer, III
Printing Coordinator: Cathy Sanchez
Contributing Artists: Gina Capaldi, Sabrina Lammé, and Leilani Trollinger

2001 Printing
ISBN 1-55501-507-7   Catalog #2-038

480 Atlas Street • Brea, CA 92821 • (800) 321-4332 • www.ballard-tighe.com • e-mail: info@ballard-tighe.com

IDEA® Picture Dictionary

Contents

How to use

This shows **how to write** the letter.

These are **guide words**. Guide words tell you the first and last words on the page.

The words are in **ABC** order.

A B C D E F G H I J K L M N O P Q R S T U V W X Y Z

airplane / ant

airplane (AYR-playn)

Spanish: aeroplano, avión

Vietnamese: phi cơ

Hmong: dav hlau

Pilipino: aeroplano

Chinese: 飞机 / 飛機

French: avion

alligator (AL-uh-gay-tur)

Spanish: cocodrilo

Vietnamese: cá sấu

Hmong: kheb

Pilipino: buwaya

Chinese: 鳄鱼 / 鱷魚

French: alligator

ambulance (AM-byoo-luns)

Spanish: ambulancia

Vietnamese: xe cứu thương

Hmong: tsheb thauj mob

Pilipino: ambulansiya

Chinese: 救护车 / 救護車

French: ambulance

ankle (ANG-kul)

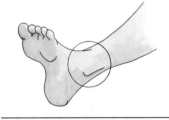

Spanish: tobillo

Vietnamese: mắt cá

Hmong: pob taws

Pilipino: bukung-bukong

Chinese: 脚脖子,踝 / 腳踝

French: cheville

ant (ant)

Spanish: hormiga

Vietnamese: con kiến

Hmong: ntsaum

Pilipino: langgam

Chinese: 蚂蚁 / 螞蟻

French: fourmi

6

this dictionary:

This is a **fun activity** for you to try.

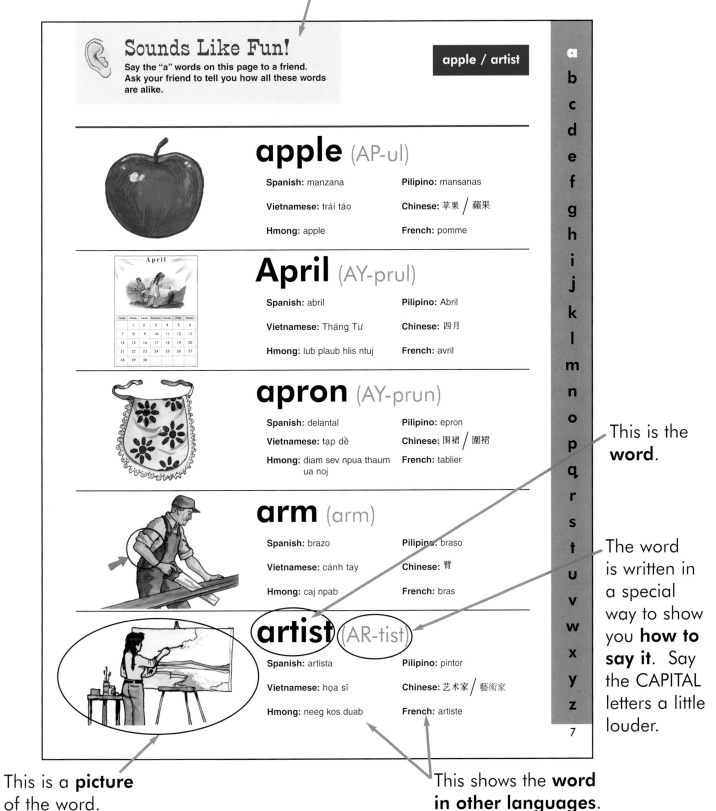

Sounds Like Fun!
Say the "a" words on this page to a friend. Ask your friend to tell you how all these words are alike.

apple / artist

apple (AP-ul)

Spanish: manzana

Pilipino: mansanas

Vietnamese: trái táo

Chinese: 苹果 / 蘋果

Hmong: apple

French: pomme

April (AY-prul)

Spanish: abril

Pilipino: Abril

Vietnamese: Tháng Tư

Chinese: 四月

Hmong: lub plaub hlis ntuj

French: avril

apron (AY-prun)

Spanish: delantal

Pilipino: epron

Vietnamese: tạp dề

Chinese: 围裙 / 圍裙

Hmong: diam sev npua thaum ua noj

French: tablier

arm (arm)

Spanish: brazo

Pilipino: braso

Vietnamese: cánh tay

Chinese: 臂

Hmong: caj npab

French: bras

artist (AR-tist)

Spanish: artista

Pilipino: pintor

Vietnamese: họa sĩ

Chinese: 艺术家 / 藝術家

Hmong: neeg kos duab

French: artiste

a b c d e f g h i j k l m n o p q r s t u v w x y z

7

This is the **word**.

The word is written in a special way to show you **how to say it**. Say the CAPITAL letters a little louder.

This is a **picture** of the word.

This shows the **word in other languages**.

5

AaAa

airplane (AYR-playn)

Spanish: aeroplano, avión

Pilipino: aeroplano

Vietnamese: phi cơ

Chinese: 飞机 / 飛機

Hmong: dav hlau

French: avion

alligator (AL-uh-gay-tur)

Spanish: cocodrilo

Pilipino: buwaya

Vietnamese: cá sấu

Chinese: 鳄鱼 / 鱷魚

Hmong: kheb

French: alligator

ambulance (AM-byoo-luns)

Spanish: ambulancia

Pilipino: ambulansiya

Vietnamese: xe cứu thương

Chinese: 救护车 / 救護車

Hmong: tsheb thauj mob

French: ambulance

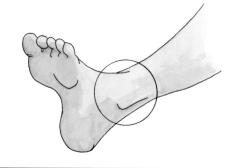

ankle (ANG-kul)

Spanish: tobillo

Pilipino: bukung-bukong

Vietnamese: mắt cá

Chinese: 脚脖子,踝 / 腳踝

Hmong: pob taws

French: cheville

ant (ant)

Spanish: hormiga

Pilipino: langgam

Vietnamese: con kiến

Chinese: 蚂蚁 / 螞蟻

Hmong: ntsaum

French: fourmi

Sounds Like Fun!

Say the "a" words on this page to a friend. Ask your friend to tell you how all these words are alike.

apple (AP-ul)

Spanish: manzana | **Pilipino:** mansanas

Vietnamese: trái táo | **Chinese:** 苹果 / 蘋果

Hmong: apple | **French:** pomme

April (AY-prul)

Spanish: abril | **Pilipino:** Abril

Vietnamese: Tháng Tư | **Chinese:** 四月

Hmong: lub plaub hlis ntuj | **French:** avril

apron (AY-prun)

Spanish: delantal | **Pilipino:** epron

Vietnamese: tạp dề | **Chinese:** 围裙 / 圍裙

Hmong: diam sev npua thaum ua noj | **French:** tablier

arm (arm)

Spanish: brazo | **Pilipino:** braso

Vietnamese: cánh tay | **Chinese:** 臂

Hmong: caj npab | **French:** bras

artist (AR-tist)

Spanish: artista | **Pilipino:** pintor

Vietnamese: họa sĩ | **Chinese:** 艺术家 / 藝術家

Hmong: neeg kos duab | **French:** artiste

a
b
c
d
e
f
g
h
i
j
k
l
m
n
o
p
q
r
s
t
u
v
w
x
y
z

astronaut (AS-truh-naht)

Spanish: astronauta   **Pilipino:** astronaut

Vietnamese: phi hành gia   **Chinese:** 太空人

Hmong: tus neeg mus saum ntuj   **French:** astronaute

August (AH-gust)

Spanish: agosto   **Pilipino:** Agosto

Vietnamese: Tháng Tám   **Chinese:** 八月

Hmong: yim hli ntuj   **French:** août

aunt (ant)

Spanish: tía   **Pilipino:** tiya

Vietnamese: cô, dì   **Chinese:** 伯母,叔母,姑妈,姨妈 / 伯母,叔母,姑媽,姨媽

Hmong: phauj, niam tais hlob, niam tais luas, niam dab laug, niam hlob, niam ntxawm   **French:** tante

axe (aks)

Spanish: hacha   **Pilipino:** palakol

Vietnamese: cái rìu   **Chinese:** 斧

Hmong: taus   **French:** hache

Bb Bb

baby (BAY-bee)

Spanish: bebé

Vietnamese: em bé

Hmong: me nyuam mos liab

Pilipino: sanggol

Chinese: 婴儿 / 嬰兒

French: bébé

back (bak)

Spanish: espalda

Vietnamese: cái lưng

Hmong: nrob qaum

Pilipino: likod

Chinese: 背

French: dos

bacon (BAY-kun)

Spanish: tocino

Vietnamese: thịt lưng heo

Hmong: nqaij sawb

Pilipino: tusino

Chinese: 熏肉 / 培根

French: lard

badge (baj)

Spanish: insignia

Vietnamese: huy hiệu

Hmong: daim ntawv coj qhia npe

Pilipino: tsapa

Chinese: 徽章

French: insigne

baker (BAY-kur)

Spanish: panadera

Vietnamese: người nướng bánh

Hmong: tus neeg ci qhaub cib thiab khoj noom

Pilipino: panadero

Chinese: 面包师 / 烤麵包師

French: boulanger

a
b
c
d
e
f
g
h
i
j
k
l
m
n
o
p
q
r
s
t
u
v
w
x
y
z

9

A
B
C
D
E
F
G
H
I
J
K
L
M
N
O
P
Q
R
S
T
U
V
W
X
Y
Z

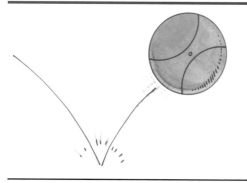

ball (bahl)

Spanish: bola, pelota **Pilipino:** bola

Vietnamese: trái banh **Chinese:** 球

Hmong: lub pob, lub npas **French:** balle

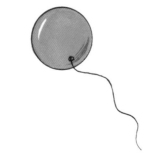

balloon (buh-LOON)

Spanish: globo **Pilipino:** lobo

Vietnamese: bong bóng **Chinese:** 汽球

Hmong: zais **French:** ballon

ballplayer
(BAHL-play-ur)

Spanish: jugador de pelota **Pilipino:** manlalaro ng bola

Vietnamese: cầu thủ **Chinese:** 球员／球員

Hmong: tus neeg ntaus pob **French:** joueur de base-ball

banana (buh-NAN-uh)

Spanish: plátano **Pilipino:** saging

Vietnamese: trái chuối **Chinese:** 香蕉

Hmong: txiv tsawb **French:** banane

bank teller
(bangk TEL-ur)

Spanish: cajera **Pilipino:** teler

Vietnamese: thư ký ngân hàng **Chinese:** 银行出纳员／銀行出納員

Hmong: tus pauv nyiaj **French:** caissier

barber (BAR-bur)

Spanish: peluquero, barbero   **Pilipino:** mangugupit

Vietnamese: thợ hớt tóc   **Chinese:** 理发师 / 理髮師

Hmong: kws txiav plaub hau   **French:** barbier, coitteur

barn (barn)

Spanish: granero   **Pilipino:** kamalig

Vietnamese: chuồng ngựa, chuồng trâu bò   **Chinese:** 谷仓 / 穀倉

Hmong: lub txhab   **French:** grange

bars (barz)

Spanish: barras   **Pilipino:** baras

Vietnamese: xà kép   **Chinese:** 杠杆 / 槓桿

Hmong: kav hlau   **French:** barres

baseball (BAYS-bahl)

Spanish: béisbol   **Pilipino:** baseball

Vietnamese: dã cầu   **Chinese:** 棒球

Hmong: lub npas cuam   **French:** base-ball

bat (bat)

Spanish: bate   **Pilipino:** talibatab

Vietnamese: cái gậy   **Chinese:** 球棒

Hmong: qws ntaus npas   **French:** batte

bat (bat)

Spanish: murciélago

Vietnamese: con dơi

Hmong: puav

Pilipino: paniki

Chinese: 蝙蝠

French: chauve-souris

bathing suit (BAY-thing soot)

Spanish: traje de baño

Vietnamese: đồ tắm

Hmong: khaub ncaws da dej

Pilipino: damit panligo

Chinese: 游泳衣

French: maillot de bain

bathroom (BATH-room)

Spanish: cuarto de baño

Vietnamese: phòng tắm

Hmong: chav dej

Pilipino: banyo, paliguan

Chinese: 浴室

French: salle de bains

bathtub (BATH-tub)

Spanish: bañera

Vietnamese: bồn tắm

Hmong: dab da dej

Pilipino: banyera

Chinese: 浴缸

French: baignoire

bean (been)

Spanish: haba, frijol

Vietnamese: đậu

Hmong: taum

Pilipino: bins

Chinese: 豆

French: haricot

A
B
C
D
E
F
G
H
I
J
K
L
M
N
O
P
Q
R
S
T
U
V
W
X
Y
Z

Sounds Like Fun!

Think of three things that start with the /b/ sound that you like to play with. Ask a partner to guess what the things are.

bear (bayr)

Spanish: oso

Pilipino: oso

Vietnamese: con gấu

Chinese: 熊

Hmong: dais

French: ours

beaver (BEE-vur)

Spanish: castor

Pilipino: castor

Vietnamese: con hải ly

Chinese: 海狸

Hmong: beaver

French: castor

bed (bed)

Spanish: cama

Pilipino: kama

Vietnamese: cái giường

Chinese: 床

Hmong: txaj

French: lit

bedroom (BED-room)

Spanish: dormitorio

Pilipino: silid-tulugan

Vietnamese: phòng ngủ

Chinese: 寝室／寢室

Hmong: chav pw

French: chambre à coucher

bee (bee)

Spanish: abeja

Pilipino: bubuyog

Vietnamese: con ong

Chinese: 蜜蜂

Hmong: muv

French: abeille

belt (belt)

Spanish: cinturón   **Pilipino:** sinturon

Vietnamese: dây nịt   **Chinese:** 皮带／皮帶

Hmong: txoj siv tawv   **French:** ceinture

bench (bench)

Spanish: banco, banca   **Pilipino:** bangko

Vietnamese: ghế dài   **Chinese:** 板凳

Hmong: lub rooj zaum   **French:** banc

bicycle (BY-sik-ul)

Spanish: bicicleta   **Pilipino:** bisikleta

Vietnamese: xe đạp   **Chinese:** 脚踏车／腳踏車

Hmong: nees zab, luv thim   **French:** bicyclette

bird (burd)

Spanish: pájaro   **Pilipino:** ibon

Vietnamese: con chim   **Chinese:** 鸟／鳥

Hmong: noog   **French:** oiseau

birthday (BURTH-day)

Spanish: cumpleaños   **Pilipino:** kaarawan

Vietnamese: sinh nhật   **Chinese:** 生日

Hmong: hnub yug   **French:** anniversaire

black (blak)

Spanish: negro

Pilipino: itim

Vietnamese: màu đen

Chinese: 黑

Hmong: dub

French: noir

block (blahk)

Spanish: cubo

Pilipino: bloke

Vietnamese: khối gỗ

Chinese: 积木／積木

Hmong: block

French: bloc

blouse (blous)

Spanish: blusa

Pilipino: blusa

Vietnamese: áo choàng

Chinese: 上衫／上衣

Hmong: tsho poj niam

French: corsage, chemisier

blue (bloo)

Spanish: azul

Pilipino: asul

Vietnamese: màu xanh

Chinese: 蓝／藍

Hmong: xiav

French: bleu

body (BAHD-ee)

Spanish: cuerpo

Pilipino: katawan

Vietnamese: cơ thể

Chinese: 身体／身體

Hmong: lub cev

French: corps

A
B
C
D
E
F
G
H
I
J
K
L
M
N
O
P
Q
R
S
T
U
V
W
X
Y
Z

book (buk)

Spanish: libro

Pilipino: aklat

Vietnamese: cuốn sách

Chinese: 书／書

Hmong: phau ntawv

French: livre

boot (boot)

Spanish: bota

Pilipino: botas

Vietnamese: giày ống

Chinese: 靴

Hmong: khau tawv

French: botte

bow and arrow
(boh and AYR-oh)

Spanish: arco y flecha

Pilipino: panalaso at pana

Vietnamese: cung và tên

Chinese: 弓 和 箭

Hmong: hneev nti thiab xib xub

French: arc et flèche

bowl (bohl)

Spanish: tazón

Pilipino: mangkok

Vietnamese: cái chén

Chinese: 碗

Hmong: tais

French: bol

boxer (BAHK-sur)

Spanish: boxeador

Pilipino: boksingero

Vietnamese: người đâú
quyền anh

Chinese: 拳师／拳師

Hmong: tus neeg ntaus nrig

French: boxeur

boy (boy)

Spanish: muchacho

Pilipino: batang lalaki

Vietnamese: bé trai

Chinese: 男孩

Hmong: tus tub

French: garçon

bracelet (BRAYS-lit)

Spanish: pulsera

Pilipino: pulseras

Vietnamese: vòng

Chinese: 手镯

Hmong: saw tes

French: bracelet

bread (bred)

Spanish: pan

Pilipino: tinapay

Vietnamese: bánh mì

Chinese: 面包 / 麵包

Hmong: qhaub cib

French: pain

breakfast (BREK-fust)

Spanish: desayuno

Pilipino: almusal

Vietnamese: bữa ăn sáng

Chinese: 早餐

Hmong: tshais

French: petit déjeuner

bridge (brij)

Spanish: puente

Pilipino: tulay

Vietnamese: cây cầu

Chinese: 桥 / 橋

Hmong: choj

French: pont

Dictionary Detective

Brown is a color. Find two other "b" words in this book that are colors.

broom (broom)

Spanish: escoba

Pilipino: walis

Vietnamese: cái chổi

Chinese: 扫帚 / 掃帚

Hmong: khaub ruab

French: balai

brother (BRUH-thur)

Spanish: hermano

Pilipino: kapatid na lalaki

Vietnamese: anh, em

Chinese: 兄弟

Hmong: tij laug, kws, nus

French: frère

brown (broun)

Spanish: marrón, café

Pilipino: kayumanggi

Vietnamese: màu nâu

Chinese: 褐色

Hmong: xim kas fes

French: marron

brush (brush)

Spanish: cepillo

Pilipino: eskoba

Vietnamese: bàn chải

Chinese: 刷

Hmong: khaub ruab

French: brosse

bucket (BUK-it)

Spanish: cubo, balde

Pilipino: timba

Vietnamese: cái xô

Chinese: 桶

Hmong: thoob

French: seau

A B C D E F G H I J K L M N O P Q R S T U V W X Y Z

buffalo (BUF-uh-loh)

Spanish: búfalo   **Pilipino:** tamaraw

Vietnamese: con bò rừng   **Chinese:** 水牛

Hmong: nyuj qus   **French:** buffle

bug (bug)

Spanish: insecto   **Pilipino:** kulisap

Vietnamese: con rêp   **Chinese:** 虫 / 蟲

Hmong: kab   **French:** punaise

bulletin board (BUL-uh-tun bord)

Spanish: tablón de anuncios   **Pilipino:** tabla ng bulitin

Vietnamese: bản thông báo   **Chinese:** 布告牌 / 公告欄

Hmong: daim ntoo lo ntawv   **French:** tableau d'affichage

bus (bus)

Spanish: autobús   **Pilipino:** bus

Vietnamese: xe buýt   **Chinese:** 公车 / 公車

Hmong: npav   **French:** autobus

bus driver (bus DRY-vur)

Spanish: conductora del autobús   **Pilipino:** tsuper ng bus

Vietnamese: tài xế xe buýt   **Chinese:** 公车司机 / 公車司機

Hmong: tus tsav npav   **French:** conducteur d'autobus

A
B
C
D
E
F
G
H
I
J
K
L
M
N
O
P
Q
R
S
T
U
V
W
X
Y
Z

bush (boosh)

Spanish: arbusto

Pilipino: halaman

Vietnamese: bụi cây

Chinese: 灌木

Hmong: nroj tsuag

French: buisson

butcher (BOOCH-ur)

Spanish: carnicero

Pilipino: mangangatay

Vietnamese: người hàng thịt

Chinese: 肉販／肉販

Hmong: tus neeg tua tsiaj thiab muag nqaij

French: boucher

butter (BUT-ur)

Spanish: mantequilla

Pilipino: mantikilya

Vietnamese: bơ

Chinese: 黄油／奶油

Hmong: butter

French: beurre

butterfly (BUT-ur-fly)

Spanish: mariposa

Pilipino: mariposa

Vietnamese: con bướm

Chinese: 蝴蝶

Hmong: npooj npaim

French: papillon

Cc

cafeteria (kaf-uh-TEER-ee-uh)

Spanish: cafetería

Vietnamese: quán ăn tự dọn

Hmong: chaw noj mov

Pilipino: kapeteriya

Chinese: 自助餐馆 / 自助餐館

French: cafétéria

cake (kayk)

Spanish: pastel

Vietnamese: bánh ngọt

Hmong: khej, ncuav qab zib

Pilipino: keyk

Chinese: 蛋糕

French: gâteau

calendar (KAL-un-dur)

Spanish: calendario

Vietnamese: lịch

Hmong: ntawv saib hnub nyoos

Pilipino: kalendaryo

Chinese: 历 / 曆

French: calendrier

calf (kaf)

Spanish: becerro

Vietnamese: con bê

Hmong: me nyuam nyuj

Pilipino: bulo

Chinese: 小牛

French: veau

camel (KAM-ul)

Spanish: camello

Vietnamese: con lạc đà

Hmong: camel

Pilipino: kamelyo

Chinese: 骆驼 / 駱駝

French: chameau

a b **c** d e f g h i j k l m n o p q r s t u v w x y z

21

camper (KAM-pur)

Spanish: vehículo para acampar

Vietnamese: xe cắm trại

Hmong: lub tsev txawb saum tsheb

Pilipino: kotse ng magkampamento

Chinese: 露营车 / 露營車

French: camping-car

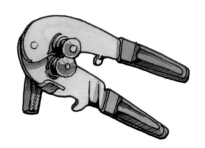

can opener
(kan OH-pun-ur)

Spanish: abrelatas

Vietnamese: cái khui đồ hộp

Hmong: tus tho kaus poom

Pilipino: abrelata

Chinese: 罐头启子 / 開罐器

French: ouvre-boîte

canoe (kuh-NOO)

Spanish: canoa

Vietnamese: thuyền

Hmong: nkoj txeeb kab

Pilipino: banka

Chinese: 独木舟 / 獨木舟

French: canoë

car (kar)

Spanish: coche

Vietnamese: xe

Hmong: tsheb

Pilipino: kotse

Chinese: 车 / 車

French: voiture

carpenter (KAR-pun-tur)

Spanish: carpintero

Vietnamese: người thợ

Hmong: neeg ua tsev

Pilipino: karpintero

Chinese: 木匠

French: charpentier

Sounds Like Fun!

Change the first letter in the word *cat* to make a new word. Make more new words just by changing the first letter. How many new words did you make?

---

carrot (KAYR-ut)

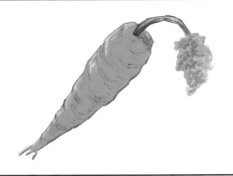

Spanish: zanahoria   **Pilipino:** karot

Vietnamese: củ cà rốt   **Chinese:** 葫萝卜 / 胡蘿蔔

Hmong: carrot   **French:** carotte

---

cat (kat)

Spanish: gato   **Pilipino:** pusa

Vietnamese: con mèo   **Chinese:** 猫 / 貓

Hmong: miv   **French:** chat

---

caterpillar (KAT-ur-pil-ur)

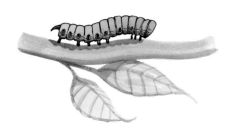

Spanish: oruga   **Pilipino:** higad

Vietnamese: con sâu   **Chinese:** 毛虫 / 毛毛蟲

Hmong: kab nyuam dev   **French:** chenille

CD (see-DEE)

Spanish: CD   **Pilipino:** CD

Vietnamese: đĩa CD   **Chinese:** 光盘 / 光碟

Hmong: CD   **French:** CD

CD player (see-DEE PLAY-ur)

Spanish: lector de CD   **Pilipino:** CD player

Vietnamese: máy CD   **Chinese:** 光盘播放机 / 光碟播放機

Hmong: lub tso CD   **French:** lecteur de CD

a b c d e f g h i j k l m n o p q r s t u v w x y z

A
B
C
D
E
F
G
H
I
J
K
L
M
N
O
P
Q
R
S
T
U
V
W
X
Y
Z

ceiling (SEEL-ing)

Spanish: techo   **Pilipino:** kisame

Vietnamese: trần nhà   **Chinese:** 天花板

Hmong: ceiling   **French:** plafond

celery (SEL-ree)

Spanish: apio   **Pilipino:** sahud

Vietnamese: cần tây   **Chinese:** 芹菜

Hmong: celery   **French:** céleri

cement mixer
(suh-MENT MIK-sur)

Spanish: mezclador del cemento   **Pilipino:** panghalo ng semento

Vietnamese: máy trộn hồ   **Chinese:** 水泥搅拌器 / 水泥攪拌器

Hmong: lub cav tov xis mas   **French:** bétonnière

cereal (SEER-ee-ul)

Spanish: cereal   **Pilipino:** seryal

Vietnamese: ngũ cốc   **Chinese:** 麦片粥 / 麥片粥

Hmong: khoj noom ntse mis **French:** céréale

chair (chayr)

Spanish: silla   **Pilipino:** silya

Vietnamese: cái ghế   **Chinese:** 椅子

Hmong: rooj zaum   **French:** chaise

chalk (chahk)

Spanish: tiza

Pilipino: tsok

Vietnamese: phấn

Chinese: 粉笔 / 粉筆

Hmong: mem av

French: craie

chalkboard (CHAHK-bord)

Spanish: pizarra

Pilipino: pisara

Vietnamese: bảng đen

Chinese: 黑板

Hmong: daim kas das

French: tableau

change (chaynj)

Spanish: cambio

Pilipino: barya

Vietnamese: đồng tiền

Chinese: 零钱 / 零錢

Hmong: nyiaj lub, nyiaj xees seen

French: monnaie

check (chek)

Spanish: cheque

Pilipino: tseke

Vietnamese: sự đinh chi

Chinese: 支票

Hmong: tshev

French: chèque

checker (CHEK-ur)

Spanish: cajera

Pilipino: tseker

Vietnamese: người giữ két

Chinese: 收银员 / 收銀員

Hmong: tus luj nqe

French: caissière

a
b
c
d
e
f
g
h
i
j
k
l
m
n
o
p
q
r
s
t
u
v
w
x
y
z

cheek (cheek)

Spanish: mejilla   **Pilipino:** pisngi

Vietnamese: cái má   **Chinese:** 颊 / 頰

Hmong: plhu   **French:** joue

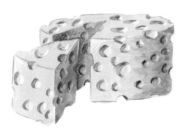

cheese (cheez)

Spanish: queso   **Pilipino:** keso

Vietnamese: phó mát   **Chinese:** 奶酪

Hmong: cheese   **French:** fromage

chemist (KEM-ist)

Spanish: química   **Pilipino:** kimiko

Vietnamese: nhà hoá học   **Chinese:** 化学家 / 化學家

Hmong: tus tov tshuaj   **French:** chimiste

cherry (CHAYR-ee)

Spanish: cereza   **Pilipino:** seresa

Vietnamese: anh đào   **Chinese:** 樱桃 / 櫻桃

Hmong: cherry   **French:** cerise

chest of drawers
(chest uv drorz)

Spanish: cómoda   **Pilipino:** kaha

Vietnamese: tủ có ngăn kéo   **Chinese:** (带抽屉的)衣橱 / 帶抽屜的衣櫥

Hmong: tub rau khaub ncaws   **French:** commode

A B C D E F G H I J K L M N O P Q R S T U V W X Y Z

Sounds Like Fun!

Take "ch" away from *chin*. Then put each of the letters of the alphabet in front of "_in." Did you make any real words? What were they?

chick (chik)

Spanish: polluelo

Pilipino: sisiw

Vietnamese: con gà con

Chinese: 小鸡 / 小雞

Hmong: me nyuam qaib

French: poussin

chicken (CHIK-un)

Spanish: pollo

Pilipino: manok

Vietnamese: con gà

Chinese: 鸡 / 雞

Hmong: qiab

French: poulet

child (chyld)

Spanish: niño

Pilipino: bata

Vietnamese: trẻ em

Chinese: 小孩

Hmong: me nyuam

French: enfant

chimney (CHIM-nee)

Spanish: chimenea

Pilipino: tsiminea

Vietnamese: ống khói

Chinese: 烟囱 / 煙囪

Hmong: chimney

French: cheminée

chin (chin)

Spanish: barbilla, mentón

Pilipino: baba

Vietnamese: cái cằm

Chinese: 下巴

Hmong: pob tsaig

French: menton

a b **c** d e f g h i j k l m n o p q r s t u v w x y z

27

chipmunk (CHIP-munk)

Spanish: ardilla listada   **Pilipino:** ardilya sa lupa

Vietnamese: con sóc chuột   **Chinese:** 花栗鼠

Hmong: nas ciav   **French:** tamia

circle (SUR-kul)

Spanish: círculo   **Pilipino:** bilog

Vietnamese: vòng tròn   **Chinese:** 圆 / 圓

Hmong: vajvoog   **French:** cercle

city (SIT-ee)

Spanish: ciudad   **Pilipino:** siyudad

Vietnamese: thành phố   **Chinese:** 都市

Hmong: lub zos   **French:** ville

clock (klahk)

Spanish: reloj   **Pilipino:** orasan

Vietnamese: đồng hồ   **Chinese:** 钟 / 鐘

Hmong: lub moos   **French:** horloge

closet (KLAHZ-it)

Spanish: armario, ropero   **Pilipino:** kloset

Vietnamese: cái tủ   **Chinese:** 壁橱

Hmong: kem tsev rau khoom   **French:** placard

a
b
c
d
e
f
g
h
i
j
k
l
m
n
o
p
q
r
s
t
u
v
w
x
y
z

clothesline (KLOHZ-lyn)

Spanish: cuerda para tender la ropa

Pilipino: sampayan

Vietnamese: dây phơi quần áo

Chinese: 晒衣绳 / 曬衣繩

Hmong: hlua ziab khaub ncaws

French: corde à linge

clothespin (KLOHZ-pin)

Spanish: pinza para tender ropa

Pilipino: sipit

Vietnamese: kẹp phơi quần áo

Chinese: 衣服夹 / 衣服夾

Hmong: pas tais khaub ncaws

French: pince à linge

clown (kloun)

Spanish: payaso

Pilipino: payaso

Vietnamese: tên hề

Chinese: 小丑

Hmong: clown

French: clown

coat (koht)

Spanish: chaqueta

Pilipino: balok

Vietnamese: áo ngoài

Chinese: 外套

Hmong: tsho tiv no

French: manteau

coffee maker (KAHF-ee MAY-kur)

Spanish: máquina de café

Pilipino: gawaan ng kape

Vietnamese: máy pha cà phê

Chinese: 咖啡器

Hmong: lub ua kas fes

French: cafetière électrique

coffeepot (KAHF-ee-paht)

Spanish: cafetera

Pilipino: lutuan ng kape

Vietnamese: bình cà phê

Chinese: 咖啡壶 / 咖啡壺

Hmong: lub rhaub kas fes

French: cafetière

colt (kohlt)

Spanish: potro

Pilipino: batang kabayo

Vietnamese: ngựa đực con

Chinese: 小马 / 小馬

Hmong: me nyuam nees

French: poulain

comb (kohm)

Spanish: peine

Pilipino: suklay

Vietnamese: cái lược

Chinese: 梳子

Hmong: zuag

French: peigne

computer (kum-PYOO-tur)

Spanish: computadora

Pilipino: komputer

Vietnamese: máy điện toán

Chinese: 电子计算机 / 電腦

Hmong: computer

French: ordinateur

cook (kuk)

Spanish: cocinero

Pilipino: kusinero, tagapagluto

Vietnamese: người đầu bếp

Chinese: 厨师 / 厨師

Hmong: tus ua zaub mov

French: cuisinier

Dictionary Detective

Find the word in this book that begins with the letter m and ends with the letter c. What word is it?

cookie (KUK-ee)

Spanish: galleta

Vietnamese: bánh

Hmong: khoj noom

Pilipino: kuki

Chinese: 饼乾 / 餅乾

French: biscuit

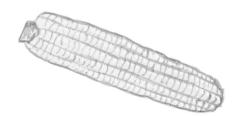

corn (korn)

Spanish: maíz, elote

Vietnamese: bắp

Hmong: pob kws

Pilipino: mais

Chinese: 玉蜀黍

French: maïs

cottage cheese (KAHT-ij cheez)

Spanish: requesón

Vietnamese: phó mát trắng

Hmong: cottage cheese

Pilipino: keso

Chinese: 农家奶酪 / 農家奶酪

French: fromage blanc

cousin (KUZ-in)

Spanish: primo

Vietnamese: người anh em họ

Hmong: kwv tij

Pilipino: pinsan

Chinese: 堂兄,弟,姊,妹

French: cousin

COW (kou)

Spanish: vaca

Vietnamese: con bò

Hmong: nyuj

Pilipino: baka

Chinese: 奶牛

French: vache

a b c d e f g h i j k l m n o p q r s t u v w x y z

31

A
B
C
D
E
F
G
H
I
J
K
L
M
N
O
P
Q
R
S
T
U
V
W
X
Y
Z

cowboy (KOU-boy)

Spanish: vaquero

Pilipino: kawboy

Vietnamese: ông chăn bò

Chinese: 牛仔

Hmong: tub zov nyuj

French: cowboy

cowgirl (KOU-gurl)

Spanish: vaquera

Pilipino: kawgirl

Vietnamese: cô gái chăn bò

Chinese: 女牛仔

Hmong: ntxhais zov nyuj

French: cowgirl

coyote (ky-OHT-ee)

Spanish: coyote

Pilipino: koyote

Vietnamese: sói đồng cỏ

Chinese: 小狼,山狗

Hmong: hma

French: coyote

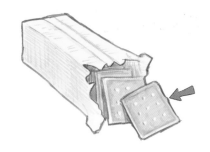

cracker (KRAK-ur)

Spanish: galleta

Pilipino: kraker

Vietnamese: bánh bích quy dòn

Chinese: 硬饼乾 / 鹹餅乾

Hmong: khoj noom

French: cracker

crane (krayn)

Spanish: grúa

Pilipino: derik

Vietnamese: máy trục

Chinese: 起重机 / 起重機

Hmong: crane

French: grue

crayon (KRAY-on)

Spanish: lápiz de cera

Pilipino: krayola

Vietnamese: viết chì màu

Chinese: 蜡笔 / 蠟筆

Hmong: xim

French: crayon de couleur

crib (krib)

Spanish: cuna

Pilipino: kuna

Vietnamese: giường giữ em bé

Chinese: 婴儿床 / 嬰兒床

Hmong: lub txoj rau me nyuam mos pw

French: lit d'enfant

cross (krahs)

Spanish: cruz

Pilipino: krus

Vietnamese: dấu chữ thập

Chinese: 十字形

Hmong: khaub lig

French: croix

cup and saucer (kup and SAH-sur)

Spanish: taza y platillo

Pilipino: tasa at platito

Vietnamese: tách và đĩa

Chinese: 杯子和茶碟

Hmong: khob thiab phaj

French: tasse et soucoupe

cupcake (KUP-kayk)

Spanish: pastelito en molde

Pilipino: kapkeyk

Vietnamese: bánh nướng hình tách

Chinese: 杯形饼 / 杯形餅

Hmong: cupcake

French: petit gâteau

a b c d e f g h i j k l m n o p q r s t u v w x y z

curve (kurv)

Spanish: curva

Pilipino: kurba

Vietnamese: đường cong

Chinese: 弯／彎

Hmong: nkhaus

French: courbe

custodian
(kus-TOH-dee-un)

Spanish: guardián

Pilipino: diyanitor

Vietnamese: người trông coi

Chinese: 清洁工／清潔工

Hmong: tus tu tsev

French: gardien

A
B
C
D
E
F
G
H
I
J
K
L
M
N
O
P
Q
R
S
T
U
V
W
X
Y
Z

dancer (DANS-ur)

Spanish: bailarina   **Pilipino:** mananayaw

Vietnamese: vũ công   **Chinese:** 舞蹈家

Hmong: tus neeg seev cev   **French:** danseur

December (dee-SEM-bur)

Spanish: diciembre   **Pilipino:** Disyembre

Vietnamese: Tháng Chạp, Tháng Mười Hai   **Chinese:** 十二月

Hmong: lub kaum ob hlis   **French:** décembre

deer (deer)

Spanish: ciervo, venado   **Pilipino:** usa

Vietnamese: con nai   **Chinese:** 鹿

Hmong: mos lwj   **French:** cerf

den (den)

Spanish: estudio   **Pilipino:** den

Vietnamese: phòng riêng nhỏ   **Chinese:** 小房

Hmong: ib hoob nyob los sis saib ntawv   **French:** petit salon

dentist (DEN-tist)

Spanish: dentista   **Pilipino:** dentista

Vietnamese: nha sĩ   **Chinese:** 牙医 / 牙醫

Hmong: kws kho hniav   **French:** dentiste

a b c **d** e f g h i j k l m n o p q r s t u v w x y z

A
B
C
D
E
F
G
H
I
J
K
L
M
N
O
P
Q
R
S
T
U
V
W
X
Y
Z

Dictionary Detective

The guide words on this page are *desk* and *dining room*. What page number has the guide words *hat* and *helicopter*?

desk (desk)

Spanish: escritorio   **Pilipino:** desk

Vietnamese: cái bàn   **Chinese:** 桌子

Hmong: rooj sau ntawv   **French:** bureau

diamond (DY-mund)

Spanish: diamante   **Pilipino:** diamante

Vietnamese: hình thoi   **Chinese:** 钻石 / 鑽石

Hmong: diamond   **French:** losange

diaper (DY-pur)

Spanish: pañal   **Pilipino:** lampin

Vietnamese: tả lót   **Chinese:** 尿布

Hmong: daiv pawm   **French:** couche

dime (dym)

Spanish: moneda de diez centavos   **Pilipino:** sampung pera

Vietnamese: đồng mười xu   **Chinese:** 一角

Hmong: kaum xees   **French:** pièce de 10 cents

dining room (DYN-ing room)

Spanish: comedor   **Pilipino:** silid kainan

Vietnamese: phòng ăn   **Chinese:** 饭厅 / 飯廳

Hmong: chav noj mov   **French:** salle à manger

36

dinner (DIN-ur)

Spanish: cena

Pilipino: hapunan

Vietnamese: bữa ăn tối

Chinese: 晚餐

Hmong: hmo

French: dîner

dinosaur (DY-nuh-sor)

Spanish: dinosaurio

Pilipino: dinosaur

Vietnamese: con khủng long

Chinese: 恐龙 / 恐龍

Hmong: dinosaur

French: dinosaure

dish (dish)

Spanish: plato

Pilipino: pinggan, plato

Vietnamese: cái dĩa

Chinese: 盘子 / 盤子

Hmong: tais diav

French: plat

dishpan (DISH-pan)

Spanish: barreño de fregar platos

Pilipino: hugasan ng pinggan

Vietnamese: bồn rửa chén dĩa

Chinese: 洗碟用盆子 / 洗碗槽

Hmong: lub tais rau tais diav

French: bassine

diskette (dihz-KET)

Spanish: disco, disquete flexible

Pilipino: diskett

Vietnamese: dĩa từ

Chinese: 磁盘, 磁碟 / 磁碟片

Hmong: diskette

French: disquette

doctor (DAHK-tur)

Spanish: médica

Pilipino: doktor

Vietnamese: bác sĩ

Chinese: 医师／醫師

Hmong: kws kho mob

French: docteur

dog (dahg)

Spanish: perro

Pilipino: aso

Vietnamese: con chó

Chinese: 狗

Hmong: aub, dev

French: chien

doll (dahl)

Spanish: muñeca

Pilipino: manyika

Vietnamese: búp bê

Chinese: 玩偶

Hmong: me nyuam roj hmab

French: poupée

dollar bill (DAHL-ur bil)

Spanish: dólar

Pilipino: isang dolyar

Vietnamese: tờ giấy bạc

Chinese: 一元纸钞／一元紙鈔

Hmong: nyiaj duas las

French: billet d'un dollar

dollhouse (DAHL-hous)

Spanish: casa de muñecas

Pilipino: bahay bahayan

Vietnamese: nhà búp bê

Chinese: 玩偶屋

Hmong: tsev ua si rau me nyam roj hmab

French: maison de poupée

dolphin (DAHL-fin)

Spanish: delfín

Vietnamese: cá heo

Hmong: dolphin

Pilipino: dolpin

Chinese: 海豚

French: dauphin

door (dor)

Spanish: puerta

Vietnamese: cánh cửa

Hmong: qhov rooj

Pilipino: pintuan

Chinese: 门 / 門

French: porte

dot (daht)

Spanish: punto

Vietnamese: dấu chấm

Hmong: ib tee

Pilipino: tuldok

Chinese: 点 / 點

French: point

doughnut (DOH-nut)

Spanish: dona

Vietnamese: bánh ngọt

Hmong: doughnut

Pilipino: donat

Chinese: 面包圈 / 甜甜圈

French: beignet

dress (dres)

Spanish: vestido

Vietnamese: áo đầm

Hmong: tiab txuas tsho

Pilipino: bestida

Chinese: 洋装 / 洋裝

French: robe

a
b
c
d
e
f
g
h
i
j
k
l
m
n
o
p
q
r
s
t
u
v
w
x
y
z

dressmaker
(DRES-may-kur)

Spanish: costurera

Vietnamese: thợ may áo quần phụ nữ

Hmong: tus neeg xaw tiab

Pilipino: mananahe

Chinese: 女裝裁縫师 / 女裝裁縫師

French: couturière

drinking fountain
(DRINK-ing FOUN-tun)

Spanish: fuente de agua potable

Vietnamese: vòi nước uống

Hmong: tus kais haus dej

Pilipino: inominang bukal

Chinese: 饮水器 / 飲水機

French: fontaine d'eau potable

drum (drum)

Spanish: tambor

Vietnamese: cái trống

Hmong: nruas

Pilipino: tambol

Chinese: 鼓

French: tambour

duck (duk)

Spanish: pato

Vietnamese: con vịt

Hmong: os

Pilipino: pato

Chinese: 鸭 / 鴨

French: canard

dustpan (DUST-pan)

Spanish: recogedor

Vietnamese: cái hốt rác

Hmong: cib laug

Pilipino: pandakot, pansaluk dumi

Chinese: 簸箕 / 畚箕

French: pelle à poussière

eagle (EE-gul)

Spanish: águila

Vietnamese: con chim ó

Hmong: dav

Pilipino: agila

Chinese: 鷹／鷹

French: aigle

ear (eer)

Spanish: oreja

Vietnamese: cái tai

Hmong: pob ntseg

Pilipino: tainga

Chinese: 耳

French: oreille

egg (eg)

Spanish: huevo

Vietnamese: cái trứng

Hmong: qe

Pilipino: itlog

Chinese: 蛋

French: oeuf

8

eight pennies

eight (ayt)

Spanish: ocho

Vietnamese: tám

Hmong: yim

Pilipino: walo

Chinese: 八

French: huit

18

eighteen snails

eighteen (ay-TEEN)

Spanish: dieciocho

Vietnamese: mười tám

Hmong: kaum yim

Pilipino: labingwalo

Chinese: 十八

French: dix-huit

a
b
c
d
e
f
g
h
i
j
k
l
m
n
o
p
q
r
s
t
u
v
w
x
y
z

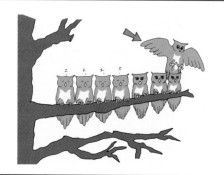

eighth (ayth)

Spanish: octavo

Vietnamese: thứ tám

Hmong: thib yim

Pilipino: pangwalo

Chinese: 第八

French: huitième

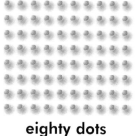

80

eighty dots

eighty (AY-tee)

Spanish: ochenta

Vietnamese: tám mươi

Hmong: yim caum

Pilipino: walumpu

Chinese: 八十

French: quatre-vingts

elbow (EL-boh)

Spanish: codo

Vietnamese: cái khủy tay

Hmong: luj tshib

Pilipino: siko

Chinese: 肘

French: coude

electrician (ih-lek-TRISH-un)

Spanish: electricista

Vietnamese: thợ điện

Hmong: tus kho hluav taws xob

Pilipino: elektrisista

Chinese: 电气技师 / 電氣技師

French: électricien

elephant (EL-uh-funt)

Spanish: elefante

Vietnamese: con voi

Hmong: ntxhw

Pilipino: elepante

Chinese: 象

French: éléphant

Sounds Like Fun!

Read aloud the "e" words on this page and clap as you say each syllable. How many words have only one syllable? How many have two? How many have three?

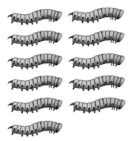

11

eleven (EE-lev-un)

eleven caterpillars

Spanish: once

Vietnamese: mười một

Hmong: kaum ib

Pilipino: labing-isa

Chinese: 十一

French: onze

e-mail (EE-mayl)

Spanish: correo electrónico

Vietnamese: thư điện tử

Hmong: e-mail

Pilipino: e-mail

Chinese: 电子邮件 / 電子郵件

French: courrier électronique

engineer (en-juh-NEER)

Spanish: ingeniero

Vietnamese: kỹ sư

Hmong: engineer

Pilipino: inhinyero

Chinese: 工程师 / 工程師

French: ingénieur

eraser (ee-RAY-sur)

Spanish: borrador

Vietnamese: cục tẩy

Hmong: lub lwv ntawv

Pilipino: pambura

Chinese: 橡皮

French: gomme

eye (I)

Spanish: ojo

Vietnamese: con mắt

Hmong: qhov muag

Pilipino: mata

Chinese: 眼

French: œil

a
b
c
d
e
f
g
h
i
j
k
l
m
n
o
p
q
r
s
t
u
v
w
x
y
z

eyebrow (I-brou)

Spanish: ceja

Pilipino: kilay

Vietnamese: lông mày

Chinese: 眉毛

Hmong: plaub muag theem saum toj

French: sourcil

eyelash (I-lash)

Spanish: pestaña

Pilipino: pilik mata

Vietnamese: lông mi

Chinese: 睫毛

Hmong: pluab muag

French: cil

eyelid (I-lid)

Spanish: párpado

Pilipino: takup mata

Vietnamese: mí mắt

Chinese: 眼皮

Hmong: tawv muag

French: paupière

face (fays)

Spanish: cara

Vietnamese: cái mặt

Hmong: ntsej muag

Pilipino: mukha

Chinese: 脸／臉

French: visage

fall (fahl)

Spanish: otoño

Vietnamese: mùa thu

Hmong: lub caij nplooj ntoos zeeg

Pilipino: taglagas

Chinese: 秋

French: automne

family (FAM-lee)

Spanish: familia

Vietnamese: gia đình

Hmong: tsev neeg

Pilipino: pamilya

Chinese: 家族

French: famille

family room
(FAM-lee room)

Spanish: cuarto de estar

Vietnamese: phòng gia đình

Hmong: chav tsev neeg nyob

Pilipino: silid pamilya

Chinese: 起居室

French: salle de séjour

fan (fan)

Spanish: ventilador

Vietnamese: cái quạt

Hmong: kiv cua

Pilipino: bentilador

Chinese: 电风扇／電風扇

French: ventilateur

a b c d e **f** g h i j k l m n o p q r s t u v w x y z

45

farmer (FAR-mur)

Spanish: granjero

Pilipino: magsasaka

Vietnamese: nông gia

Chinese: 农夫／農夫

Hmong: tswv teb, neeg ua liag ua teb

French: fermier

father (FAH-thur)

Spanish: padre

Pilipino: ama

Vietnamese: cha

Chinese: 父亲／父親

Hmong: txiv

French: père

fawn (fahn)

Spanish: cervato

Pilipino: batang usa

Vietnamese: con hươu con

Chinese: 小鹿

Hmong: me nyuam mos lwj

French: faon

February (FEB-yoo-ayr-ee)

Spanish: febrero

Pilipino: Pebrero

Vietnamese: Tháng Hai

Chinese: 二月

Hmong: lub ob hlis

French: février

15

fifteen ladybugs

fifteen (fif-TEEN)

Spanish: quince

Pilipino: labinlima

Vietnamese: mười lăm

Chinese: 十五

Hmong: kaum tsib

French: quinze

A B C D E **F** G H I J K L M N O P Q R S T U V W X Y Z

fifth (fifth)

Spanish: quinto **Pilipino:** panlima

Vietnamese: thứ năm **Chinese:** 第五

Hmong: thib tsib **French:** cinquième

fifty (FIF-tee)

50

fifty dots

Spanish: cincuenta **Pilipino:** limampu

Vietnamese: năm mươi **Chinese:** 五十

Hmong: tsib caug **French:** cinquante

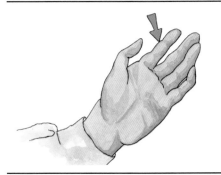

finger (FING-ur)

Spanish: dedo **Pilipino:** daliri

Vietnamese: ngón tay **Chinese:** 手指

Hmong: ntiv tes **French:** doigt

fingernail
(FING-ur-nayl)

Spanish: uña **Pilipino:** kuko

Vietnamese: móng tay **Chinese:** 指甲

Hmong: rau tes **French:** ongle

fire engine (fyr EN-jun)

Spanish: coche de bomberos **Pilipino:** trak ng bombero

Vietnamese: xe cứu hỏa **Chinese:** 消防车／消防車

Hmong: tsheb tua hluav taws **French:** voiture de pompiers

A
B
C
D
E
F
G
H
I
J
K
L
M
N
O
P
Q
R
S
T
U
V
W
X
Y
Z

Dictionary Detective

Find the first "w" word in this book. What word is it?

firefighter (FYR-fyt-ur)

Spanish: bombero   **Pilipino:** bombero

Vietnamese: lính cứu hỏa   **Chinese:** 消防員／消防員

Hmong: neeg tua hluav taws   **French:** pompier

first (furst)

Spanish: primero   **Pilipino:** una

Vietnamese: thứ nhứt   **Chinese:** 第一

Hmong: thib ib   **French:** premier

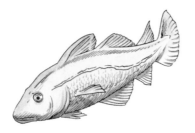

fish (fish)

Spanish: pez   **Pilipino:** isda

Vietnamese: con cá   **Chinese:** 鱼／魚

Hmong: ntses   **French:** poisson

five (fyv)

five blocks

Spanish: cinco   **Pilipino:** lima

Vietnamese: năm   **Chinese:** 五

Hmong: tsib   **French:** cinq

flag (flag)

Spanish: bandera   **Pilipino:** watawat

Vietnamese: lá cờ   **Chinese:** 旗

Hmong: chij   **French:** drapeau

floor (flor)

Spanish: piso

Vietnamese: sàn nhà

Hmong: lub plag tsev

Pilipino: sahig

Chinese: 地板

French: sol

flower (FLOU-ur)

Spanish: flor

Vietnamese: bông hoa

Hmong: lub paj

Pilipino: bulaklak

Chinese: 花

French: fleur

fly (fly)

Spanish: mosca

Vietnamese: con ruồi

Hmong: yoov

Pilipino: langaw

Chinese: 苍蝇／蒼蠅

French: mouche

foot (fut)

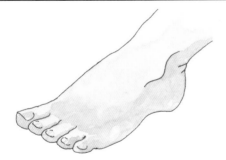

Spanish: pie

Vietnamese: cái bàn chân

Hmong: taw

Pilipino: paa

Chinese: 脚／腳

French: pied

football (FUT-bahl)

Spanish: pelota de fútbol

Vietnamese: túc cầu

Hmong: football

Pilipino: putbol

Chinese: 足球

French: ballon de football américain

a
b
c
d
e
f
g
h
i
j
k
l
m
n
o
p
q
r
s
t
u
v
w
x
y
z

A
B
C
D
E
F
G
H
I
J
K
L
M
N
O
P
Q
R
S
T
U
V
W
X
Y
Z

forehead (FOR-hed)

Spanish: frente

Vietnamese: cái trán

Hmong: hauv pliaj

Pilipino: noo

Chinese: 额 / 額頭

French: front

fork (fork)

Spanish: tenedor

Vietnamese: cái nĩa

Hmong: diav rawg

Pilipino: tinidor

Chinese: 又

French: fourchette

40

forty dots

forty (FOR-tee)

Spanish: cuarenta

Vietnamese: bốn mươi

Hmong: plaub caug

Pilipino: apatnapu

Chinese: 四十

French: quarante

 4

four balloons

four (for)

Spanish: cuatro

Vietnamese: bốn

Hmong: plaub

Pilipino: apat

Chinese: 四

French: quatre

14

fourteen spiders

fourteen (for-TEEN)

Spanish: catorce

Vietnamese: mười bốn

Hmong: kaum plaub

Pilipino: labing-apat

Chinese: 十四

French: quatorze

50

fourth (forth)

Spanish: cuarto

Vietnamese: thứ tư

Hmong: thib plaub

Pilipino: pangapat

Chinese: 第四

French: quatrième

fox (fahks)

Spanish: zorro

Vietnamese: con chồn

Hmong: hma

Pilipino: soro

Chinese: 狐

French: renard

Friday (FRY-day)

Spanish: viernes

Vietnamese: Thứ Sáu

Hmong: Friday

Pilipino: Biyernes

Chinese: 星期五

French: vendredi

frog (frahg)

Spanish: rana

Vietnamese: con ếch

Hmong: qav̌

Pilipino: palaka

Chinese: 青蛙

French: grenouille

frying pan (FRY-ing pan)

Spanish: sartén

Vietnamese: cái chảo

Hmong: lub yias

Pilipino: kawali

Chinese: 炒锅 / 炒鍋

French: poêle

a b c d e **f** g h i j k l m n o p q r s t u v w x y z

Gg Gg

game (gaym)

Spanish: juego
Pilipino: laro

Vietnamese: trò chơi
Chinese: 游戏 / 遊戲

Hmong: kev ua si
French: jeu

gardener (GARD-nur)

Spanish: jardinero
Pilipino: hardinero

Vietnamese: người làm vườn
Chinese: 园丁 / 園丁

Hmong: neej tus vaj
French: jardinier

giraffe (juh-RAF)

Spanish: jirafa
Pilipino: hirapa

Vietnamese: hươu cao cổ
Chinese: 长颈鹿 / 長頸鹿

Hmong: nees caj dab ntev
French: girafe

girl (gurl)

Spanish: muchacha
Pilipino: batang babae

Vietnamese: con gái
Chinese: 女孩

Hmong: tus ntxhais
French: fille

glass (glas)

Spanish: vaso
Pilipino: baso

Vietnamese: cái ly
Chinese: 玻璃

Hmong: khob iav
French: verre

glasses (GLAS-iz)

Spanish: gafas, anteojos, lentes   **Pilipino:** salamin sa mata

Vietnamese: kính đeo mắt   **Chinese:** 眼镜 / 眼鏡

Hmong: lub tsom qhov muag   **French:** lunettes

globe (glohb)

Spanish: globo terráqueo   **Pilipino:** globo

Vietnamese: quả địa cầu   **Chinese:** 地球仪 / 地球儀

Hmong: lub ntiaj teb   **French:** globe

glove (gluv)

Spanish: guante   **Pilipino:** guwantes

Vietnamese: găng tay   **Chinese:** 手套

Hmong: hnab looj tes   **French:** gant

glue (gloo)

Spanish: pegamento   **Pilipino:** pandikit

Vietnamese: keo dán   **Chinese:** 胶 / 膠

Hmong: kua nplaum   **French:** colle

goat (goht)

Spanish: cabra   **Pilipino:** kambing

Vietnamese: con dê   **Chinese:** 山羊

Hmong: tus tshis   **French:** chèvre

a b c d e f **g** h i j k l m n o p q r s t u v w x y z

Sounds Like Fun!

Complete this sentence with a "g" word: "The girl gave her grandmother a ___." Now ask some friends to finish the sentence with other "g" words.

goose (goos)

Spanish: ganso

Pilipino: gansa

Vietnamese: con ngỗng

Chinese: 鹅／鵝

Hmong: os quab

French: oie

gorilla (guh-RIL-uh)

Spanish: gorila

Pilipino: gurilya

Vietnamese: con khỉ đột

Chinese: 大猩猩

Hmong: ib hom liab

French: gorille

grandfather (GRAND-fah-thur)

Spanish: abuelo

Pilipino: ingkong, lolo

Vietnamese: ông nội, ông ngoại

Chinese: 祖父

Hmong: yawg

French: grand-père

grandmother (GRAND-muh-thur)

Spanish: abuela

Pilipino: impo, lola

Vietnamese: bà nội, bà ngoại

Chinese: 祖母

Hmong: pog

French: grand-mère

grape (grayp)

Spanish: uva

Pilipino: ubas

Vietnamese: trái nho

Chinese: 葡萄

Hmong: grape

French: raisin

A B C D E F G H I J K L M N O P Q R S T U V W X Y Z

grapefruit (GRAYP-froot)

Spanish: pomelo, toronja

Vietnamese: trái bưởi

Hmong: txiv lws zoov

Pilipino: suha

Chinese: 柚子

French: pamplemousse

grass (gras)

Spanish: hierba, césped

Vietnamese: cỏ

Hmong: nyom

Pilipino: damo

Chinese: 草

French: herbe

grasshopper (GRAS-hahp-ur)

Spanish: saltamontes

Vietnamese: con châu chấu

Hmong: kooj txig

Pilipino: tipaklong

Chinese: 蚱蜢

French: sauterelle

green (green)

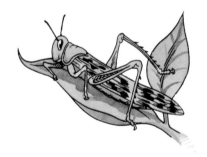

Spanish: verde

Vietnamese: màu xanh lá cây

Hmong: ntsuab

Pilipino: berde

Chinese: 绿 / 綠

French: vert

guitar (gih-TAR)

Spanish: guitarra

Vietnamese: lục huyền cầm

Hmong: kiv taj, teev tee

Pilipino: gitara

Chinese: 吉他

French: guitare

a
b
c
d
e
f
g
h
i
j
k
l
m
n
o
p
q
r
s
t
u
v
w
x
y
z

gum (gum)

Spanish: goma de mascar, chicle

Vietnamese: nướu răng, kẹo cao su

Hmong: khoj noom yas

Pilipino: gum

Chinese: 橡皮糖／口香糖

French: gomme à mâcher, chewing gum

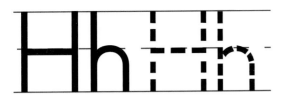

hair (hayr)

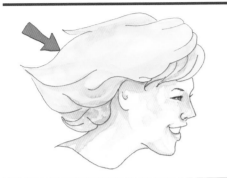

Spanish: pelo

Vietnamese: tóc

Hmong: plaub hau

Pilipino: buhok

Chinese: 头发 / 頭髮

French: cheveux

hairbrush (HAYR-brush)

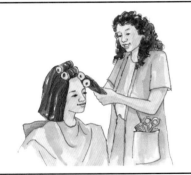

Spanish: cepillo para el pelo

Vietnamese: bàn chải tóc

Hmong: zuag ntsis plaubhau

Pilipino: eskoba ng buhok

Chinese: 发刷 / 髮刷

French: brosse à chevaux

hairdresser (HAYR-dres-ur)

Spanish: peinadora

Vietnamese: thợ cắt tóc

Hmong: tus kho plaubhau

Pilipino: tagapagkulot

Chinese: 美发师 / 美髮師

French: coiffeur

half-dollar (haf-DAHL-ur)

Spanish: medio dólar

Vietnamese: nửa mỹ kim

Hmong: lub nyiaj tsib caug xees

Pilipino: kalahati ng dolyar

Chinese: 半块钱 / 半塊錢

French: pièce de cinquante cents

half-hour (haf-OUR)

Spanish: media hora

Vietnamese: nửa giờ

Hmong: peb caug nas this

Pilipino: kalahating oras

Chinese: 半小时 / 半小時

French: demi-heure

A
B
C
D
E
F
G
H
I
J
K
L
M
N
O
P
Q
R
S
T
U
V
W
X
Y
Z

half past (haf past)

half past 2 o'clock

Spanish: dos y media

Pilipino: ... i media

Vietnamese: nửa giờ sau

Chinese: 过了半··· / 過了牛···

Hmong: peb caug nas this dhau

French: et demi

ham (ham)

Spanish: jamón

Pilipino: hamon

Vietnamese: thịt heo

Chinese: 火腿

Hmong: ib hom nqaij

French: jambon

hamburger (HAM-bur-gur)

Spanish: hamburguesa

Pilipino: hamburger

Vietnamese: bánh mì mềm kẹp thịt bằm

Chinese: 煎牛肉饼 / 漢堡

Hmong: hamburger

French: hamburger

hammer (HAM-ur)

Spanish: martillo

Pilipino: martilyo

Vietnamese: cái búa

Chinese: 锤 / 鎚

Hmong: rauj

French: marteau

hand (hand)

Spanish: mano

Pilipino: kamay

Vietnamese: bàn tay

Chinese: 手

Hmong: tes

French: main

hat (hat)

Spanish: sombrero

Pilipino: sumbrero

Vietnamese: cái mũ

Chinese: 帽子

Hmong: kos mom

French: chapeau

head (hed)

Spanish: cabeza

Pilipino: ulo

Vietnamese: cái đầu

Chinese: 头 / 頭

Hmong: taub hau

French: tête

heater (HEET-ur)

Spanish: calentador

Pilipino: panginit

Vietnamese: lò sưởi

Chinese: 暖气 / 暖氣機

Hmong: lub tso pa sov

French: appareil de chauffage

heel (heel)

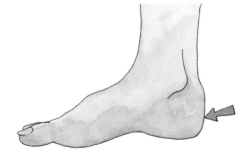

Spanish: talón

Pilipino: sakong

Vietnamese: gót chân

Chinese: 后脚跟 / 後脚跟

Hmong: pob taws

French: talon

helicopter
(HEL-ih-kahp-tur)

Spanish: helicóptero

Pilipino: helikopter

Vietnamese: máy bay trực thăng

Chinese: 直升飞机 / 直昇飛機

Hmong: nyuj hoom qav taub

French: hélicoptère

a
b
c
d
e
f
g
h
i
j
k
l
m
n
o
p
q
r
s
t
u
v
w
x
y
z

Dictionary Detective

Hen and *horse* are animals. What is the only word in this book that is an animal which begins with the letter z?

hen (hen)

Spanish: gallina

Vietnamese: con gà mái

Hmong: poj qaib

Pilipino: inahin

Chinese: 母鸡 / 母雞

French: poule

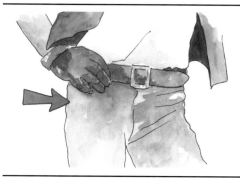

hip (hip)

Spanish: cadera

Vietnamese: cái hông

Hmong: ntshag

Pilipino: balakang

Chinese: 臀部

French: hanche

hippopotamus (hip-uh-PAHT-uh-mus)

Spanish: hipopótamo

Vietnamese: con hà mã

Hmong: npua dej

Pilipino: hipopotamus

Chinese: 河马 / 河馬

French: hippopotame

hoe (hoh)

Spanish: azada, azadón

Vietnamese: cái cuốc

Hmong: hlau

Pilipino: asarol

Chinese: 镐 / 鈀

French: binette, pioche, bêche

horse (hors)

Spanish: caballo

Vietnamese: con ngựa

Hmong: nees

Pilipino: kabayo

Chinese: 马 / 馬

French: cheval

A
B
C
D
E
F
G
H
I
J
K
L
M
N
O
P
Q
R
S
T
U
V
W
X
Y
Z

hose (hohz)

Spanish: manguera

Vietnamese: ống nước

Hmong: hlua dej, xaim dej

Pilipino: gomang pandilig

Chinese: 水管

French: tuyau

hot dog (HAHT dahg)

Spanish: perro caliente

Vietnamese: xúc xích

Hmong: nyuv txwm

Pilipino: hotdog

Chinese: 热狗 / 熱狗

French: hot-dog

hour (our)

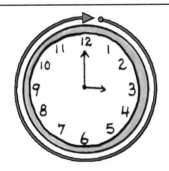

Spanish: hora

Vietnamese: giờ đồng hồ

Hmong: xuam moos

Pilipino: oras

Chinese: 小时 / 小時

French: heure

hour hand (our hand)

hour hand

Spanish: manilla de reloj

Vietnamese: kim chỉ giờ

Hmong: tus tes qhia xuam moos

Pilipino: maikling kamay ng relo

Chinese: 时针 / 時針

French: petite aiguille

a
b
c
d
e
f
g
h
i
j
k
l
m
n
o
p
q
r
s
t
u
v
w
x
y
z

61

A
B
C
D
E
F
G
H
I
J
K
L
M
N
O
P
Q
R
S
T
U
V
W
X
Y
Z

ice cream (iz kreem)

Spanish: helado

Vietnamese: cà rem

Hmong: kee lees

Pilipino: sorbetes

Chinese: 冰淇淋

French: glace

ice skate (iz skayt)

Spanish: patín del hielo

Vietnamese: giày trượt băng

Hmong: ice skate

Pilipino: isket sa yelo

Chinese: 滑冰 / 滑冰

French: patin à glace

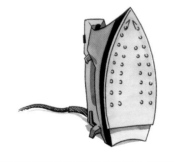

Internet (IN-tur-net)

Spanish: Internet

Vietnamese: liên mạng

Hmong: eevthawsnem

Pilipino: Internet

Chinese: 国际互联网 / 網際網路

French: Internet

iron (I-urn)

Spanish: plancha

Vietnamese: cái bàn ủi

Hmong: lus luam khaub ncaws

Pilipino: plantsa

Chinese: 熨斗

French: fer à repasser

ironing board (I-urn-ing bord)

Spanish: mesa de planchar

Vietnamese: bàn có lót nệm để ủi

Hmong: daim txiag luam khaub ncaws

Pilipino: plantsahan

Chinese: 熨衣板

French: planche à repasser, table à repasser

62

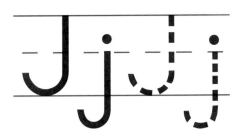

jacket (JAK-it)

Spanish: chaqueta **Pilipino:** diyaket

Vietnamese: áo khoát ngoài **Chinese:** 夹克 / 夾克

Hmong: tsho tiv no **French:** veste

jam (jam)

Spanish: mermelada **Pilipino:** halaya

Vietnamese: mứt **Chinese:** 果酱 / 果醬

Hmong: jam **French:** confiture

January (JAN-yoo-ayr-ee)

Spanish: enero **Pilipino:** Enero

Vietnamese: Tháng Giêng **Chinese:** 一月

Hmong: ib hlis **French:** janvier

jaw (jah)

Spanish: quijada **Pilipino:** panga

Vietnamese: cái hàm **Chinese:** 颚 / 顎

Hmong: puab tsaig **French:** mâchoire

jeep (jeep)

Spanish: jeep **Pilipino:** dyip

Vietnamese: xe gíp **Chinese:** 吉普车 / 吉普車

Hmong: tsheb, jeep **French:** jeep

a b c d e f g h i **j** k l m n o p q r s t u v w x y z

A B C D E F G H I J K L M N O P Q R S T U V W X Y Z

jello (JEL-oh)

Spanish: gelatina   **Pilipino:** gulaman

Vietnamese: món thạch đông   **Chinese:** 果冻 / 果凍

Hmong: jello   **French:** am gelée

jelly (JEL-ee)

Spanish: jalea, mermelada   **Pilipino:** halaya

Vietnamese: thạch đông   **Chinese:** 果酱 / 果醬

Hmong: ntsiavlim   **French:** gelée

jet (jet)

Spanish: avión de reacción   **Pilipino:** dyet

Vietnamese: phản lực cơ   **Chinese:** 喷射机 / 噴射機

Hmong: davhlau   **French:** avion à réaction

judge (juj)

Spanish: juez   **Pilipino:** hukom

Vietnamese: thẩm phán   **Chinese:** 法官

Hmong: tus txiav txim   **French:** juge

juice (joos)

Spanish: jugo   **Pilipino:** katas

Vietnamese: nước trái cây   **Chinese:** 果汁

Hmong: kua txiv ntoo   **French:** jus

Dictionary Detective

Jump rope is made of two words: *jump* and *rope*. Find five other words that are made of two words. What are they?

July (juh-LY)

Spanish: julio

Pilipino: Hulyo

Vietnamese: Tháng Bảy

Chinese: 七月

Hmong: xya hlis

French: juillet

jump rope (jump rohp)

Spanish: saltador, cuerda de saltar

Pilipino: talon lubid

Vietnamese: dây để nhảy

Chinese: 跳绳 / 跳繩

Hmong: txoj hlua dhia

French: corde à sauter

June (joon)

Spanish: junio

Pilipino: Hunyo

Vietnamese: Tháng Sáu

Chinese: 六月

Hmong: rau hlis

French: juin

a
b
c
d
e
f
g
h
i
j
k
l
m
n
o
p
q
r
s
t
u
v
w
x
y
z

Kk

A B C D E F G H I J **K** L M N O P Q R S T U V W X Y Z

kangaroo
(kang-guh-ROO)

Spanish: canguro   **Pilipino:** kanggaro

Vietnamese: con đại thử   **Chinese:** 袋鼠

Hmong: kangaroo   **French:** kangourou

key (kee)

Spanish: llave   **Pilipino:** susi

Vietnamese: chìa khóa   **Chinese:** 钥匙 / 鑰匙

Hmong: yawm sij, kas ces   **French:** clef

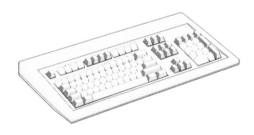

keyboard (KEE-bord)

Spanish: teclado   **Pilipino:** teklado

Vietnamese: bàn phím chữ   **Chinese:** 键盘 / 鍵盤

Hmong: keyboard   **French:** clavier

king (king)

Spanish: rey   **Pilipino:** hari

Vietnamese: ông vua   **Chinese:** 国王 / 國王

Hmong: huab tais   **French:** roi

kitchen (KICH-un)

Spanish: cocina   **Pilipino:** kusina

Vietnamese: nhà bếp   **Chinese:** 厨房 / 廚房

Hmong: chav ua noj   **French:** cuisine

kite (kyt)

Spanish: cometa

Vietnamese: con diều

Hmong: lub khaij

Pilipino: saranggola

Chinese: 鸢,风筝 / 風箏

French: cerf-volant

kitten (KIT-un)

Spanish: gatito

Vietnamese: con mèo con

Hmong: me nyuam miv

Pilipino: kuting

Chinese: 小猫 / 小貓

French: chaton

knee (nee)

Spanish: rodilla

Vietnamese: đầu gối

Hmong: hauv caug

Pilipino: tuhod

Chinese: 膝盖 / 膝蓋

French: genou

knife (nyf)

Spanish: cuchillo

Vietnamese: con dao

Hmong: riam

Pilipino: lanseta

Chinese: 刀

French: couteau

a
b
c
d
e
f
g
h
i
j
k
l
m
n
o
p
q
r
s
t
u
v
w
x
y
z

A
B
C
D
E
F
G
H
I
J
K
L
M
N
O
P
Q
R
S
T
U
V
W
X
Y
Z

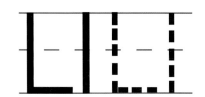

ladder (LAD-ur)

Spanish: escalera

Pilipino: hagdan

Vietnamese: cái thang

Chinese: 梯子

Hmong: ntaiv

French: échelle

ladybug (LAYD-ee-bug)

Spanish: mariquita

Pilipino: kulisap

Vietnamese: con bọ hung

Chinese: 瓢虫 / 瓢蟲

Hmong: kab huab txhib

French: coccinelle

lake (layk)

Spanish: lago

Pilipino: lawa

Vietnamese: cái hồ

Chinese: 湖

Hmong: lub pas dej

French: lac

lamb (lam)

Spanish: cordero

Pilipino: kordero

Vietnamese: con cừu non

Chinese: 小羊

Hmong: me nyuam yaj

French: agneau

lamp (lamp)

Spanish: lámpara

Pilipino: ilawan

Vietnamese: cái đèn

Chinese: 灯 / 檯燈

Hmong: lub teeb

French: lampe

Sounds Like Fun!

Think of three things that start with the /l/ sound. Ask a partner to guess what they are.

leg / lettuce

leg (leg)

Spanish: pierna

Vietnamese: cái chân

Hmong: txhais ceg

Pilipino: pata

Chinese: 腿

French: jambe

lemon (LEM-un)

Spanish: limón

Vietnamese: trái chanh

Hmong: mas naus

Pilipino: limon

Chinese: 柠檬 / 檸檬

French: citron

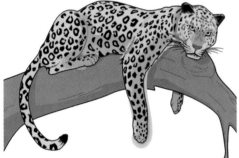

leopard (LEP-urd)

Spanish: leopardo

Vietnamese: con báo

Hmong: tsov txaij

Pilipino: leopard

Chinese: 豹

French: léopard

letter (LET-ur)

Spanish: carta

Vietnamese: lá thư

Hmong: tsab ntawv

Pilipino: liham

Chinese: 书信 / 書信

French: lettre

lettuce (LET-us)

Spanish: lechuga

Vietnamese: rau diếp

Hmong: zaub qhwv

Pilipino: litsugas

Chinese: 萵苣

French: laitue

a b c d e f g h i j k **l** m n o p q r s t u v w x y z

69

A
B
C
D
E
F
G
H
I
J
K
L
M
N
O
P
Q
R
S
T
U
V
W
X
Y
Z

librarian
(ly-BRAYR-ee-un)

Spanish: bibliotecaria   **Pilipino:** laybraryan

Vietnamese: quản thủ thư viện   **Chinese:** 图书馆员 / 圖書館員

Hmong: tus saib tsev nyeem ntawv   **French:** bibliothécaire

library (LY-brayr-ee)

Spanish: biblioteca   **Pilipino:** aklatan

Vietnamese: thư viện   **Chinese:** 图书馆 / 圖書館

Hmong: tsev nyeem ntawv   **French:** bibliothèque

lifeguard (LYF-gard)

Spanish: salvavidas   **Pilipino:** tagapagligtas

Vietnamese: người cứu đắm   **Chinese:** 救生员 / 救生員

Hmong: tus saib kom txob muaj neeg poob deg   **French:** maître nageur

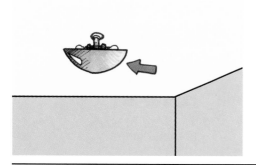

light (lyt)

Spanish: luz   **Pilipino:** ilaw

Vietnamese: ánh sáng, đèn   **Chinese:** 灯光 / 燈光

Hmong: teeb   **French:** lumière

line (lyn)

Spanish: línea   **Pilipino:** linya

Vietnamese: đường   **Chinese:** 线 / 線

Hmong: txoj kab   **French:** ligne

lion (LY-un)

Spanish: león

Vietnamese: con sư tử

Hmong: tso ntxhuav

Pilipino: leon

Chinese: 狮子 / 獅子

French: lion

lip (lip)

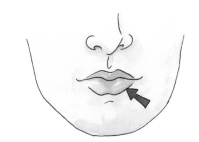

Spanish: labio

Vietnamese: môi

Hmong: de ncauj

Pilipino: labi

Chinese: 唇

French: lèvre

living room (LIV-ing room)

Spanish: sala de estar

Vietnamese: phòng khách

Hmong: chav nyob

Pilipino: salas

Chinese: 起居室

French: salle

lizard (LIZ-urd)

Spanish: lagarto

Vietnamese: con rắn mối

Hmong: nab qa

Pilipino: lagarto

Chinese: 蜥蜴

French: lézard

lobster (LAHB-stur)

Spanish: langosta

Vietnamese: con tôm hùm

Hmong: cws

Pilipino: ulang

Chinese: 龙虾 / 龍蝦

French: homard

a b c d e f g h i j k **l** m n o p q r s t u v w x y z

lock (lahk)

Spanish: candado, cerradura   **Pilipino:** kandado

Vietnamese: ổ khóa   **Chinese:** 锁 / 鎖

Hmong: ntsuas poo   **French:** cadenas

lunch (lunch)

Spanish: almuerzo   **Pilipino:** tanghalian

Vietnamese: bữa ăn trưa   **Chinese:** 午餐

Hmong: su   **French:** déjeuner

Mm Mm

magazine
(MAG-uh-zeen)

Spanish: revista

Pilipino: magasin

Vietnamese: tạp chí

Chinese: 杂志 / 雜誌

Hmong: magazine

French: magazine

mail carrier
(mayl KAYR-ee-ur)

Spanish: cartera

Pilipino: kartero

Vietnamese: người phát thư

Chinese: 邮递员 / 郵遞員

Hmong: tus neeg nqa ntawv

French: facteur

mail truck (mayl truk)

Spanish: carro del correo

Pilipino: trak ng koreo

Vietnamese: xe thư

Chinese: 邮递开车 / 郵遞卡車

Hmong: lub tsheb xa ntawv

French: fourgonnette des postes

man (man)

Spanish: hombre

Pilipino: lalaki

Vietnamese: người đàn ông

Chinese: 男子

Hmong: txiv neej

French: homme

map (map)

Spanish: mapa

Pilipino: mapa

Vietnamese: bản đồ

Chinese: 地图 / 地圖

Hmong: pheem thib

French: carte

a b c d e f g h i j k l **m** n o p q r s t u v w x y z

Dictionary Detective

Find the only word in this book that begins with the letter i and ends with the letter m. What word is it?

March (march)

Spanish: marzo   **Pilipino:** Marso

Vietnamese: Tháng Ba   **Chinese:** 三月

Hmong: peb hlis ntuj   **French:** mars

May (may)

Spanish: mayo   **Pilipino:** Mayo

Vietnamese: Tháng Năm   **Chinese:** 五月

Hmong: tsib hlis ntuj   **French:** mai

meat (meet)

Spanish: carne   **Pilipino:** karne

Vietnamese: thịt   **Chinese:** 肉

Hmong: nqaij   **French:** viande

mechanic (muh-KAN-ik)

Spanish: mecánico   **Pilipino:** mekaniko

Vietnamese: thợ máy   **Chinese:** 机械工 / 機械工

Hmong: tus khos tsheb   **French:** mécanicien

microwave oven
(MY-kroh-wayv UV-un)

Spanish: microonda   **Pilipino:** microwave oven

Vietnamese: lò vi ba   **Chinese:** 微波炉 / 微波爐

Hmong: qhov cub hluav taws xob   **French:** four à micro-ondes

a b c d e f g h i j k l **m** n o p q r s t u v w x y z

milk (milk)

Spanish: leche

Pilipino: gatas

Vietnamese: sữa

Chinese: 牛奶

Hmong: mis nyuj

French: lait

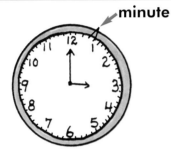

minute

minute (MIN-it)

Spanish: minuto

Pilipino: minuto

Vietnamese: phút

Chinese: 分

Hmong: nas thi

French: minute

minute hand

minute hand
(MIN-it hand)

Spanish: minutero

Pilipino: mahabang kamay ng relo

Vietnamese: kim chỉ phút

Chinese: 分针 / 分針

Hmong: tus tes qhia nas thi

French: grande aiguille

mirror (MEER-ur)

Spanish: espejo

Pilipino: salamin

Vietnamese: gương soi

Chinese: 镜 / 鏡

Hmong: daim iav

French: miroir

mitten (MIT-un)

Spanish: guante, mitón

Pilipino: guwantes

Vietnamese: găng hở ngón

Chinese: 手套

Hmong: hnab loog tes

French: mouffle

moccasin
(MAHK-uh-sun)

Spanish: mocasín   **Pilipino:** mokasin

Vietnamese: giày da đế bẹt   **Chinese:** 平底鞋

Hmong: ib hom khau   **French:** mocassin

Monday (MUN-day)

Spanish: lunes   **Pilipino:** Lunes

Vietnamese: Thứ Hai   **Chinese:** 星期一

Hmong: Monday   **French:** lundi

monitor (MAHN-ih-tur)

Spanish: monitór   **Pilipino:** monitor

Vietnamese: máy quan sát   **Chinese:** 屏幕 / 電腦螢幕

Hmong: monitor   **French:** moniteur

monkey (MUN-kee)

Spanish: mono   **Pilipino:** unggoy

Vietnamese: con khỉ   **Chinese:** 猴

Hmong: tus liab   **French:** singe

moose (moos)

Spanish: alce   **Pilipino:** anta

Vietnamese: con một loài hươu   **Chinese:** 麋鹿

Hmong: moose   **French:** orignal

mop (mahp)

Spanish: trapeador, fregona

Pilipino: panlampaso

Vietnamese: cây lau nhà

Chinese: 拖把

Hmong: tus txhuam tsev

French: serpillière

mosquito (muh-SKEET-oh)

Spanish: mosquito

Pilipino: lamok

Vietnamese: con muỗi

Chinese: 蚊

Hmong: yoov tshaj cum

French: moustique

mother (MUH-thur)

Spanish: madre

Pilipino: ina

Vietnamese: mẹ

Chinese: 母亲 / 母親

Hmong: niam

French: mère

motorcycle (MOH-tur-sy-kul)

Spanish: motocicleta

Pilipino: motorsiklo

Vietnamese: xe gắn máy

Chinese: 机器脚踏车 / 摩托車

Hmong: mau taus

French: moto

mouse (mous)

Spanish: ratón

Pilipino: daga

Vietnamese: con chuột

Chinese: 鼠

Hmong: tus nas

French: souris

a b c d e f g h i j k l **m** n o p q r s t u v w x y z

A
B
C
D
E
F
G
H
I
J
K
L
M
N
O
P
Q
R
S
T
U
V
W
X
Y
Z

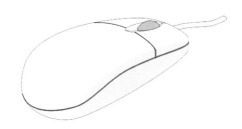

mouse (mous)

Spanish: ratón de computadora
Pilipino: mouse
Vietnamese: con chuột
Chinese: 鼠标器 / 鼠標器
Hmong: mouse
French: souris

mouth (mouth)

Spanish: boca
Pilipino: bibig
Vietnamese: cái miệng
Chinese: 嘴
Hmong: qhov ncauj
French: bouche

moving van (MOO-ving van)

Spanish: camión de mudanzas
Pilipino: trak ng paglipat
Vietnamese: xe van dọn nhà
Chinese: 搬家卡车 / 搬家卡車
Hmong: tsheb thauj khoom tsiv
French: camion de déménagement

musician (myoo-ZISH-un)

Spanish: músico
Pilipino: musikero
Vietnamese: nhạc sĩ
Chinese: 音乐家 / 音樂家
Hmong: neeg ntau nruas tshuab raj
French: musicien

nail (nayl)

Spanish: clavo

Vietnamese: cái đinh

Hmong: ntsia hlau

Pilipino: pako

Chinese: 钉子 / 釘子

French: clou

napkin (NAP-kin)

Spanish: servilleta

Vietnamese: khăn lau

Hmong: ntawv thiab ntaub so ncauj

Pilipino: serbilyeta

Chinese: 餐巾

French: serviette

neck (nek)

Spanish: cuello

Vietnamese: cái cổ

Hmong: caj dab

Pilipino: leeg

Chinese: 颈 / 頸

French: cou

necklace (NEK-lis)

Spanish: collar

Vietnamese: dây chuyền

Hmong: saw caj dab

Pilipino: kuwintas

Chinese: 项链 / 項鍊

French: collier

news carrier
(nooz KAYR-ee-ur)

Spanish: repartidor de periódicos

Vietnamese: người phát báo

Hmong: tus xas ntawv

Pilipino: mensahero

Chinese: 送报员 / 送報員

French: livreur de journaux

a b c d e f g h i j k l m **n** o p q r s t u v w x y z

Sounds Like Fun!

What number word do you see in *nineteen* and *ninety*? If you said, "nine," you are right. Think of other number words you can put in front of "___teen" and "___ty." What new words can you make?

newspaper
(NOOZ-pay-pur)

Spanish: periódico, diario

Vietnamese: báo chí

Hmong: ntawv xov xum

Pilipino: diyaryo

Chinese: 报纸 / 報紙

French: journal

nickel (NIK-ul)

Spanish: moneda de cinco centavos

Vietnamese: đồng năm xu

Hmong: tsib xees

Pilipino: limang sentimos

Chinese: 五分钱 / 五分錢

French: pièce de cinq cents

9

nine bananas

nine (nyn)

Spanish: nueve

Vietnamese: chín

Hmong: cuaj

Pilipino: siyam

Chinese: 九

French: neuf

19

nineteen cherries

nineteen (nyn-TEEN)

Spanish: diecinueve

Vietnamese: mười chín

Hmong: kaum cuaj

Pilipino: labinsiyam

Chinese: 十九

French: dix-neuf

90

ninety dots

ninety (NYN-tee)

Spanish: noventa

Vietnamese: chín mươi

Hmong: cuaj caum

Pilipino: siyamnapu

Chinese: 九十

French: quatre-vingt-dix

ninth (nynth)

Spanish: noveno

Pilipino: ikasiyam

Vietnamese: thứ chín

Chinese: 第九

Hmong: thib cuaj

French: neuvième

nose (nohz)

Spanish: nariz

Pilipino: ilong

Vietnamese: cái mũi

Chinese: 鼻

Hmong: taub ntswm

French: nez

November (noh-VEM-bur)

Spanish: noviembre

Pilipino: Nobyembre

Vietnamese: Tháng Mười Một

Chinese: 十一月

Hmong: kaum ib hlis ntuj

French: novembre

nurse (nurs)

Spanish: enfermera

Pilipino: nars

Vietnamese: y tá

Chinese: 护士 ／ 護士

Hmong: nurse

French: infirmière

nut (nut)

Spanish: nuez

Pilipino: mane

Vietnamese: đậu phụng

Chinese: 坚果 ／ 堅果

Hmong: noob txiv ntoo

French: noix

a b c d e f g h i j k l m **n** o p q r s t u v w x y z

A B C D E F G H I J K L M N **O** P Q R S T U V W X Y Z

O o **O o**

---

ocean (OH-shun)

Spanish: océano   **Pilipino:** karagatan

Vietnamese: đại dương   **Chinese:** 海洋

Hmong: dej hiav txwv, dej ntuj   **French:** océan

October (ahk-TOH-bur)

Spanish: octubre   **Pilipino:** Oktubre

Vietnamese: Tháng Mười   **Chinese:** 十月

Hmong: kaum hli ntuj   **French:** octobre

---

octopus (AHK-tuh-pus)

Spanish: pulpo   **Pilipino:** oktopus

Vietnamese: con bạch tuộc   **Chinese:** 章鱼 / 章魚

Hmong: octopus   **French:** pieuvre

---

office (AHF-is)

Spanish: oficina   **Pilipino:** opisina

Vietnamese: văn phòng   **Chinese:** 办公室 / 辦公室

Hmong: chaw ua hauj lwm   **French:** bureau

---

one (wun)

1

one soccer ball

Spanish: uno   **Pilipino:** isa

Vietnamese: một   **Chinese:** 一

Hmong: ib   **French:** un

one hundred
(wun HUN-dred)

100

one hundred dots

Spanish: cien	**Pilipino:** isandaan
Vietnamese: một trăm	**Chinese:** 一百
Hmong: ib puas	**French:** cent

onion (UN-yen)

Spanish: cebolla	**Pilipino:** sibuyas
Vietnamese: củ hành	**Chinese:** 洋葱
Hmong: lub dos loj	**French:** oignon

orange (OR-inj)

Spanish: naranja	**Pilipino:** mamulamulang-dilaw
Vietnamese: màu cam	**Chinese:** 橘色
Hmong: xim liab ziv, tsiv tsuav	**French:** orange

orange (OR-inj)

Spanish: naranja	**Pilipino:** dalandan
Vietnamese: trái cam	**Chinese:** 橘 / 柳橙
Hmong: txiv kab ntxwv	**French:** orange

ostrich (AHS-trich)

Spanish: avestruz	**Pilipino:** ostrik
Vietnamese: con đà điểu	**Chinese:** 鸵鸟 / 鴕鳥
Hmong: ostrich	**French:** autruche

a
b
c
d
e
f
g
h
i
j
k
l
m
n
o
p
q
r
s
t
u
v
w
x
y
z

Sounds Like Fun!

Pick a word that begins with the letter o and draw a picture for each letter in the word. For example, for *owl*, **you might draw an <u>o</u>nion, a <u>w</u>orm, and a <u>l</u>amp. Ask a friend to guess the word by looking at your picture.**

oval (OH-vul)

Spanish: oval

Vietnamese: hình bầu dục

Hmong: oval

Pilipino: obalo

Chinese: 椭圆形 / 橢圓形

French: ovale

owl (oul)

Spanish: búho

Vietnamese: con cú

Hmong: tus plas

Pilipino: kuwago

Chinese: 猫头鹰 / 貓頭鷹

French: hibou

A B C D E F G H I J K L M N O P Q R S T U V W X Y Z

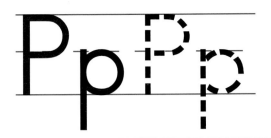

page (payj)

Spanish: página

Vietnamese: trang giấy

Hmong: phab ntawv

Pilipino: pahina

Chinese: 页 / 頁

French: page

pail (payl)

Spanish: cubo

Vietnamese: cái xô

Hmong: lub thoob

Pilipino: timba

Chinese: 桶

French: seau

painter (PAYNT-ur)

Spanish: pintor

Vietnamese: thợ sơn

Hmong: tus pleev xim

Pilipino: pintor

Chinese: 油漆工

French: peintre

pajamas (puh-JAH-muhz)

Spanish: pijamas

Vietnamese: áo quần ngủ

Hmong: kob ncaws hnav pw

Pilipino: padyama

Chinese: 睡衣

French: pyjamas

pan (pan)

Spanish: cacerola

Vietnamese: cái nôi

Hmong: lauj kaub

Pilipino: kawali

Chinese: 锅 / 鍋

French: casserole

A
B
C
D
E
F
G
H
I
J
K
L
M
N
O
P
Q
R
S
T
U
V
W
X
Y
Z

pancake (PAN-kayk)

Spanish: crepe, tortita, panqueque

Vietnamese: bánh kếp

Hmong: pancake

Pilipino: pankeyk

Chinese: 薄烤饼 / 薄烤餅

French: crêpe

pants (pants)

Spanish: pantalones

Vietnamese: cái quần

Hmong: lub ris

Pilipino: pantalon

Chinese: 裤 / 褲

French: pantalon

paper (PAY-pur)

Spanish: papel

Vietnamese: giấy

Hmong: daim ntawv

Pilipino: papel

Chinese: 纸 / 紙

French: papier

parrot (PAYR-ut)

Spanish: loro

Vietnamese: con vẹt

Hmong: leeb nkaub

Pilipino: loro

Chinese: 鹦鹉 / 鸚鵡

French: perroquet

paste (payst)

Spanish: engrudo

Vietnamese: bột nhão

Hmong: kua nplaum

Pilipino: pandikit

Chinese: 糊

French: pâte

a b c d e f g h i j k l m n o **p** q r s t u v w x y z

patio (PAT-ee-oh)

Spanish: patio

Pilipino: patiyo

Vietnamese: hiên nhà

Chinese: 平台 / 陽台

Hmong: lawj (siab)

French: patio

pea (pee)

Spanish: guisante

Pilipino: gisantes

Vietnamese: đậu xanh

Chinese: 豌豆

Hmong: noob taum pauv

French: pois

peacock (PEE-kahk)

Spanish: pavo real

Pilipino: paboreal

Vietnamese: con công

Chinese: 孔雀

Hmong: noog yaj yuam

French: paon

peanut butter
(PEE-nut BUT-ur)

Spanish: manteca de cacahuete, manteca de maní

Pilipino: mantikilya ng mani

Vietnamese: bơ đậu phụng

Chinese: 花生酱 / 花生醬

Hmong: txiv laum huab zeeb zom

French: beurre de cacahuètes

pear (payr)

Spanish: pera

Pilipino: peras

Vietnamese: trái lê

Chinese: 梨子

Hmong: pear

French: poire

pencil (PEN-sul)

Spanish: lápiz

Vietnamese: bút chì

Hmong: xom

Pilipino: lapis

Chinese: 铅笔 / 鉛筆

French: crayon

pencil sharpener
(PEN-sul SHAR-puh-nur)

Spanish: sacapuntas de lápiz

Vietnamese: máy bào bút chì

Hmong: lub hliav xom

Pilipino: pantasa

Chinese: 转笔刀 / 削鉛筆機

French: taille-crayons

penguin (PENG-gwin)

Spanish: pingüino

Vietnamese: chim cánh ngắn

Hmong: penguin

Pilipino: pengguwin

Chinese: 企鹅 / 企鵝

French: pingouin, manchot

penny (PEN-ee)

Spanish: centavo

Vietnamese: đồng xu

Hmong: lub ib xeev

Pilipino: isang pera

Chinese: 一分 / 一分錢

French: pièce de 1 cent

pharmacist
(FAR-muh-sist)

Spanish: farmacéutico

Vietnamese: dược sĩ

Hmong: tus kws tshuaj

Pilipino: parmaseutiko

Chinese: 药剂师 / 藥劑師

French: pharmacien

piano (pee-AN-oh)

Spanish: piano   **Pilipino:** piyano

Vietnamese: dương cầm   **Chinese:** 钢琴 / 鋼琴

Hmong: piano   **French:** piano

pie (py)

Spanish: pastel   **Pilipino:** pay

Vietnamese: bánh ba tê   **Chinese:** 馅饼 / 餡餅

Hmong: lub phais   **French:** tarte

pig (pig)

Spanish: cerdo   **Pilipino:** baboy

Vietnamese: con heo   **Chinese:** 猪

Hmong: tus npua   **French:** porc

pilot (PY-lut)

Spanish: piloto   **Pilipino:** piloto

Vietnamese: phi công   **Chinese:** 飞机驾驶员 / 飛機駕駛員

Hmong: tus tsav dav hlau **French:** pilote

piñata (pee-NYAH-tah)

Spanish: piñata   **Pilipino:** pinyata

Vietnamese: gói đồ chơi treo   **Chinese:** 墨西哥生日玩具
lên để đập bể
dịp lễ

Hmong: piñata   **French:** piñata

A
B
C
D
E
F
G
H
I
J
K
L
M
N
O
P
Q
R
S
T
U
V
W
X
Y
Z

pineapple (PYN-ap-ul)

Spanish: piña

Pilipino: pinya

Vietnamese: trái thơm

Chinese: 菠萝 / 鳳梨

Hmong: txiv puv luj

French: ananas

plate (playt)

Spanish: plato

Pilipino: plato

Vietnamese: cái đĩa

Chinese: 盘 / 盤

Hmong: phaj

French: assiette

playground (PLAY-ground)

Spanish: campo de juegos

Pilipino: palaruan

Vietnamese: sân chơi

Chinese: 游戏场地 / 遊戲場地

Hmong: chaw ua si

French: cour de jeu, cour de récréation

plumber (PLUM-ur)

Spanish: plomero, fontanero

Pilipino: plomero

Vietnamese: thợ ống nước

Chinese: 铅工 / 鉛工

Hmong: kws kho dej

French: plombier

polar bear (POH-lur bayr)

Spanish: oso polar

Pilipino: oso na galing sa mayelong lugar

Vietnamese: con gấu trắng

Chinese: 北极熊 / 北極熊

Hmong: dais dawb

French: ours blanc, ours polaire

police car
(puh-LEES kar)

Spanish: coche de policía

Pilipino: kotse ng pulis

Vietnamese: xe cảnh sát

Chinese: 警车／警車

Hmong: tub ceev xwm tsheb

French: voiture de police

police officer
(puh-LEES AH-fis-ur)

Spanish: agente de policía

Pilipino: opisyal ng pulis

Vietnamese: cảnh sát viên

Chinese: 警察

Hmong: tus ceev xwm

French: officier de police, policier

popcorn (PAHP-korn)

Spanish: palomitas

Pilipino: binusang mais

Vietnamese: bắp rang dòn

Chinese: 爆米花

Hmong: paj kws

French: pop-corn

porch (porch)

Spanish: pórtico

Pilipino: portiko

Vietnamese: hiên nhà

Chinese: 门口／門口

Hmong: lawj (qis)

French: porche

porcupine
(POR-kyuh-pyn)

Spanish: puerco espín

Pilipino: porkoespin

Vietnamese: con nhím

Chinese: 豪猪

Hmong: tsaug

French: porc-épic

a b c d e f g h i j k l m n o **p** q r s t u v w x y z

91

potato (puh-TAY-toh)

Spanish: patata, papa

Vietnamese: khoai tây

Hmong: qos yaj ywm

Pilipino: patatas

Chinese: 土豆 / 馬鈴薯

French: pomme de terre

potato chip (puh-TAY-toh chip)

Spanish: papas fritas

Vietnamese: lát khoai tây chiên dòn

Hmong: potato chip

Pilipino: potato tsip

Chinese: 油炸土豆片 / 洋芋片

French: chips

president (PREZ-uh-dunt)

Spanish: presidente

Vietnamese: tổng thống

Hmong: tus nom

Pilipino: pangulo

Chinese: 总统 / 總統

French: président

principal (PRIN-suh-pul)

Spanish: directora

Vietnamese: hiệu trưởng

Hmong: tus thaw hauv tsev kawm ntawv

Pilipino: punong-guro

Chinese: 校长 / 校長

French: principal

pumpkin (PUMP-kin)

Spanish: calabaza

Vietnamese: bí ngô

Hmong: taub

Pilipino: kalabasa

Chinese: 南瓜

French: potiron

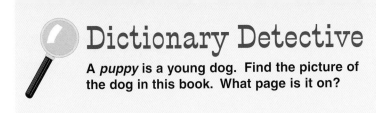

Dictionary Detective

A *puppy* is a young dog. Find the picture of the dog in this book. What page is it on?

puppy (PUP-ee)

Spanish: perrito

Pilipino: tuta

Vietnamese: con chó con

Chinese: 小狗

Hmong: me nyuam aub, me nyuam dev

French: chiot

purple (PUR-pul)

Spanish: morado, violeta

Pilipino: purpura

Vietnamese: màu tím

Chinese: 紫红色

Hmong: tsam xem

French: violet

purse (purs)

Spanish: monedero, bolsa

Pilipino: portamoneda

Vietnamese: cái bóp xách tay

Chinese: 钱包／錢包

Hmong: hnab nqa ntawm tes, kas paus

French: sac à main

a b c d e f g h i j k l m n o **p** **q** r s t u v w x y z

93

Qq Qq

quarter (KWORT-ur)

Spanish: moneda de 25 centavos

Pilipino: ikaapat

Vietnamese: đồng hai mười lăm xu

Chinese: 二毛五

Hmong: lub nyiaj nees nkaum tsib xees

French: pièce de 25 cents

quarter past 8 o'clock

quarter past (KWORT-ur past)

Spanish: … y quarto

Pilipino: menos kinse

Vietnamese: quá mười lăm phút

Chinese: 过十五分 / 過十五分

Hmong: kaum tsib na thi dhau

French: et quart

quarter to 5 o'clock

quarter to (till) (KWORT-ur too [til])

Spanish: un cuarto para las…

Pilipino: para

Vietnamese: kém mười lăm phút (đến)

Chinese: 差十五分

Hmong: tshuav kaum tsib na thi

French: moins le quart

queen (kween)

Spanish: reina

Pilipino: reyna

Vietnamese: nữ hoàng

Chinese: 女王

Hmong: poj huab tais

French: reine

A B C D E F G H I J K L M N O P **Q** R S T U V W X Y Z

a b c d e f g h i j k l m n o p q **r** s t u v w x y z

rabbit (RAB-it)

Spanish: conejo

Pilipino: kuneho

Vietnamese: con thỏ

Chinese: 兔子

Hmong: tus luav

French: lapin

raccoon (ra-KOON)

Spanish: mapache

Pilipino: rakoon

Vietnamese: con gấu trúc

Chinese: 浣熊

Hmong: ntshuab

French: raton laveur

racing car (RAYS-ing kar)

Spanish: coche de carreras

Pilipino: kotseng pangkarera

Vietnamese: xe đua

Chinese: 赛车 / 賽車

Hmong: tsheb sib xeem

French: voiture de course

radio (RAY-dee-oh)

Spanish: radio

Pilipino: radio

Vietnamese: máy thu thanh

Chinese: 收音机 / 收音機

Hmong: xov tooj cua

French: radio

raincoat (RAYN-koht)

Spanish: impermeable

Pilipino: kapote

Vietnamese: áo mưa

Chinese: 雨衣

Hmong: tsho tiv nag

French: imperméable

Sounds Like Fun!

Rake rhymes with *cake*. Now it's your turn to make a rhyme. Think of a word that rhymes with *rat*. Ask a partner to guess the word.

---

rake (rayk)

Spanish: rastrillo

Vietnamese: cái cào

Hmong: pas hus nroj tsuag

Pilipino: kalaykay

Chinese: 耙子

French: râteau

---

rat (rat)

Spanish: rata

Vietnamese: con chuột

Hmong: nas tsuag

Pilipino: daga

Chinese: 鼠

French: rat

---

rectangle (REK-tayng-ul)

Spanish: rectángulo

Vietnamese: hình chữ nhật

Hmong: rectangle

Pilipino: parihaba

Chinese: 长方形 / 長方形

French: rectangle

---

red (red)

Spanish: rojo

Vietnamese: màu đỏ

Hmong: liab

Pilipino: pula

Chinese: 红 / 紅

French: rouge

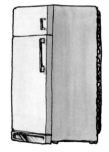

refrigerator
(rih-FRIJ-uh-ray-tur)

Spanish: refrigerador

Vietnamese: cái tủ lạnh

Hmong: tub yees

Pilipino: pridyeder

Chinese: 冰箱

French: réfrigérateur

rhinoceros
(ry-NAHS-ur-us)

Spanish: rinoceronte   **Pilipino:** rinoseros

Vietnamese: con tê giác   **Chinese:** 犀牛

Hmong: twj kum   **French:** rhinocéros

rice (rys)

Spanish: arroz   **Pilipino:** kanin

Vietnamese: cơm   **Chinese:** 米

Hmong: mov   **French:** riz

ring (ring)

Spanish: anillo   **Pilipino:** singsing

Vietnamese: cái nhẫn   **Chinese:** 戒指

Hmong: nplhaib   **French:** bague

river (RIV-ur)

Spanish: río   **Pilipino:** ilog

Vietnamese: con sông   **Chinese:** 河川

Hmong: tus dej   **French:** fleuve, rivière

road (rohd)

Spanish: carretera   **Pilipino:** daan

Vietnamese: con đường   **Chinese:** 道路

Hmong: txoj kev   **French:** route

a b c d e f g h i j k l m n o p q r s t u v w x y z

robe (rohb)

Spanish: bata

Vietnamese: áo choàng

Hmong: lub tsho hnav npog

Pilipino: balabal

Chinese: 长外袍 / 長外袍

French: peignoir

rocket (RAHK-it)

Spanish: cohete

Vietnamese: hỏa tiển

Hmong: cua luaj

Pilipino: raket

Chinese: 火箭

French: fusée

roller skate
(ROHL-ur skayt)

Spanish: patín de ruedas

Vietnamese: giày có bánh xe để trượt

Hmong: khau log

Pilipino: gulong na isket, roler isket

Chinese: 旱冰鞋 / 溜冰鞋

French: patin à roulettes

roof (roof)

Spanish: techo, tejado

Vietnamese: mái nhà

Hmong: ru tsev

Pilipino: bubong

Chinese: 屋顶 / 屋頂

French: toit

room (room)

Spanish: sala, salón

Vietnamese: căn phòng

Hmong: chav, hoob

Pilipino: kuwarto

Chinese: 房间 / 房間

French: salle

rooster (ROOS-tur)

Spanish: gallo

Pilipino: tandang

Vietnamese: con gà trống

Chinese: 雄鸡 / 雄雞

Hmong: lau qaib

French: coq

ruler (ROO-lur)

Spanish: regla

Pilipino: reglador

Vietnamese: cái thước

Chinese: 尺

Hmong: pas ntsuas

French: règle

Ss Ss

sailboat (SAYL-boht)

Spanish: barco de vela

Pilipino: batel

Vietnamese: thuyền buồm

Chinese: 帆船

Hmong: nko cua

French: bateau à voiles

salad (SAL-ud)

Spanish: ensalada

Pilipino: salad

Vietnamese: rau xà lách

Chinese: 生菜沙拉

Hmong: xa lav

French: salade

sales clerk (SAYLZ klurk)

Spanish: vendedor

Pilipino: tindera

Vietnamese: ngươi bán hàng

Chinese: 店员 / 店員

Hmong: tus muag khoom

French: vendeur

salt (sahlt)

Spanish: sal

Pilipino: asin

Vietnamese: muối

Chinese: 盐 / 鹽

Hmong: ntsev

French: sel

sandbox (SAND-bahks)

Spanish: cajón de arena

Pilipino: larnan ng buhangin

Vietnamese: hộp cát

Chinese: 沙盒

Hmong: thawv xuab zeeb

French: bac à sable

Dictionary Detective

Saturday is one of the days of the week. Look at the table of contents. Which page tells you <u>all</u> the days of the week?

---

sandwich (SAND-wich)

Spanish: emparedado   **Pilipino:** sanwits

Vietnamese: bánh mì săn quých   **Chinese:** 三明治

Hmong: sandwich   **French:** sandwich

Saturday (SAT-ur-day)

Spanish: sábado   **Pilipino:** Sabado

Vietnamese: Thứ Bảy   **Chinese:** 星期六

Hmong: Saturday   **French:** samedi

---

saw (sah)

Spanish: sierra, serrucho   **Pilipino:** lagari

Vietnamese: cái cưa   **Chinese:** 锯子 / 鋸子

Hmong: kaw   **French:** scie

---

school bus (SKOOL bus)

Spanish: autobús escolar   **Pilipino:** bus na pangeskuwela

Vietnamese: xe buýt học đường   **Chinese:** 校车 / 校車

Hmong: npav thauj me nyuam kawm ntawv   **French:** autobus scolaire

---

scissors (SIZ-urz)

Spanish: tijeras   **Pilipino:** gunting

Vietnamese: cái kéo   **Chinese:** 剪刀

Hmong: rab txiab   **French:** ciseaux

a b c d e f g h i j k l m n o p q r **s** t u v w x y z

sea (see)

Spanish: mar

Pilipino: dagat

Vietnamese: biển

Chinese: 海

Hmong: dej hiav txwv

French: mer

sea horse (SEE hors)

Spanish: caballo de mar

Pilipino: kabayong-dagat

Vietnamese: con hải mã

Chinese: 海马／海馬

Hmong: nees dej

French: hippocampe

seal (seel)

Spanish: foca

Pilipino: poka

Vietnamese: con hải cẩu

Chinese: 海狗

Hmong: ntshuab deg

French: phoque

sea turtle (see TUR-tul)

Spanish: tortuga del mar

Pilipino: pawikan

Vietnamese: con rùa biển

Chinese: 海龟／海龜

Hmong: vaub kib dej

French: tortue de mer

second (SEK-und)

Spanish: segundo

Pilipino: pangalawa

Vietnamese: thứ nhì

Chinese: 第二

Hmong: thib ob

French: second

a
b
c
d
e
f
g
h
i
j
k
l
m
n
o
p
q
r
s
t
u
v
w
x
y
z

secretary
(SEK-ruh-tayr-ee)

Spanish: secretaria   **Pilipino:** sekretarya

Vietnamese: thư ký   **Chinese:** 秘书／秘書

Hmong: tus khaws ntaub ntawv   **French:** secrétaire

September
(sep-TEM-bur)

Spanish: septiembre   **Pilipino:** Setyembre

Vietnamese: Tháng Chín   **Chinese:** 九月

Hmong: cuaj hli ntuj   **French:** septembre

7

seven (SEV-un)

Spanish: siete   **Pilipino:** pito

Vietnamese: bảy   **Chinese:** 七

Hmong: xya   **French:** sept

seven tops

17

seventeen
(sev-un-TEEN)

Spanish: diecisiete   **Pilipino:** labimpito

Vietnamese: mười bảy   **Chinese:** 十七

Hmong: kaum xya   **French:** dix-sept

seventeen butterflies

seventh (SEV-unth)

Spanish: séptimo   **Pilipino:** ikapito

Vietnamese: thứ bảy   **Chinese:** 第七

Hmong: thib xya   **French:** septième

seventy (SEV-un-tee)

70

seventy dots

Spanish: setenta

Vietnamese: bảy mươi

Hmong: xya caum

Pilipino: pitumpu

Chinese: 七十

French: soixante-dix

sewing machine (SOH-ing muh-SHEEN)

Spanish: máquina de costura

Vietnamese: máy may

Hmong: tshuab xaws khaub ncaws

Pilipino: makinang pangtahe

Chinese: 裁缝机 / 裁縫機

French: machine à coudre

shark (shark)

Spanish: tiburón

Vietnamese: con cá mập

Hmong: shark

Pilipino: pating

Chinese: 鲨鱼 / 鯊魚

French: requin

sheep (sheep)

Spanish: oveja

Vietnamese: con cừu

Hmong: yaj

Pilipino: tupa

Chinese: 羊

French: mouton

shell (shel)

Spanish: concha

Vietnamese: con sò

Hmong: pliag deg

Pilipino: kabibi

Chinese: 贝壳 / 貝殼

French: coquillage

A B C D E F G H I J K L M N O P Q R *S* T U V W X Y Z

Dictionary Detective

All the words on this page begin with the letters s and h. Find two words in this book that begin with "b" and end with "sh." What are they?

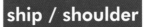

ship (ship)

Spanish: barco, buque

Pilipino: barko

Vietnamese: chiếc tàu

Chinese: 船

Hmong: lub nkoj loj

French: bateau

shirt (shurt)

Spanish: camisa

Pilipino: kamisadentro

Vietnamese: áo sơ mi

Chinese: 衬衫 / 襯衫

Hmong: lub tsho

French: chemisier, chemise

shoe (shoo)

Spanish: zapato

Pilipino: sapatos

Vietnamese: giày

Chinese: 鞋

Hmong: khau

French: chaussure

shorts (shorts)

Spanish: pantalones cortos

Pilipino: maikling pantalon

Vietnamese: quần ngắn

Chinese: 短裤 / 短褲

Hmong: ris luv

French: shorts

shoulder (SHOHL-dur)

Spanish: hombro

Pilipino: balikat

Vietnamese: cái vai

Chinese: 肩膀

Hmong: xwb pwg

French: épaule

a b c d e f g h i j k l m n o p q r **s** t u v w x y z

shovel (SHUV-ul)

Spanish: pala   **Pilipino:** pala

Vietnamese: cái xẻng   **Chinese:** 铲子 / 鏟子

Hmong: hlau yawm av, rab luab   **French:** pelle

sidewalk (SYD-wahk)

Spanish: acera   **Pilipino:** bangketa

Vietnamese: lối đi bộ   **Chinese:** 人行道

Hmong: ntug kev   **French:** trottoir

sink (sink)

Spanish: fregadero   **Pilipino:** lababo

Vietnamese: cái bồn   **Chinese:** 洗手池

Hmong: dab ntxuav tes   **French:** évier

sister (SIS-tur)

Spanish: hermana   **Pilipino:** kapatid na babae

Vietnamese: chị, em gái   **Chinese:** 姊妹

Hmong: niam laus, niam hluas, viv ncaus, muam   **French:** sœur

6

six strawberries

six (siks)

Spanish: seis   **Pilipino:** anim

Vietnamese: sáu   **Chinese:** 六

Hmong: rau   **French:** six

16

sixteen flies

sixteen (siks-TEEN)

Spanish: dieciséis

Pilipino: labing-anim

Vietnamese: mười sáu

Chinese: 十六

Hmong: kaum rau

French: seize

sixth (siksth)

Spanish: sexto

Pilipino: ikaanim

Vietnamese: thứ sáu

Chinese: 第六

Hmong: thib rau

French: sixième

60

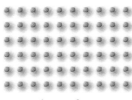

sixty dots

sixty (SIKS-tee)

Spanish: sesenta

Pilipino: animnapu

Vietnamese: sáu mươi

Chinese: 六十

Hmong: rau caum

French: soixante

skateboard (SKAYT-bord)

Spanish: patineta, monopatín

Pilipino: isketbord

Vietnamese: ván trượt

Chinese: 溜冰板

Hmong: skateboard

French: planche à roulettes

skin (skin)

Spanish: piel

Pilipino: balat

Vietnamese: da

Chinese: 皮肤 / 皮膚

Hmong: tawv nqaij

French: peau

a b c d e f g h i j k l m n o p q r s t u v w x y z

A B C D E F G H I J K L M N O P Q R **S** T U V W X Y Z

skirt (skurt)

Spanish: falda

Pilipino: saya

Vietnamese: cái váy

Chinese: 裙子

Hmong: daim tiab

French: jupe

skunk (skunk)

Spanish: zorrillo, mofeta

Pilipino: mabahong hayop kapag nagulat

Vietnamese: con chồn hôi

Chinese: 臭鼬鼠

Hmong: skunk

French: moufette

sky (sky)

Spanish: cielo

Pilipino: langit

Vietnamese: bầu trời

Chinese: 天空

Hmong: saum ntuj

French: ciel

slide (slyd)

Spanish: resbaladero

Pilipino: magpadulas

Vietnamese: ván trượt

Chinese: 滑板 / 溜滑梯

Hmong: zawv zawg

French: toboggan

slipper (SLIP-ur)

Spanish: pantufla, zapatilla

Pilipino: tsinelas

Vietnamese: dép lê

Chinese: 拖鞋

Hmong: khau rau hauv tsev

French: pantoufle

Sounds Like Fun!

Go on a two-minute word hunt with a friend. Start the clock and in two minutes find as many things as you can that start with the letter s.

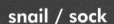

snail (snayl)

Spanish: caracol

Vietnamese: con ốc sên

Hmong: qwj yeeg

Pilipino: kuhol

Chinese: 蜗牛 / 蝸牛

French: escargot

snake (snayk)

Spanish: serpiente

Vietnamese: con rắn

Hmong: nab

Pilipino: ahas

Chinese: 蛇

French: serpent

soap (sohp)

Spanish: jabón

Vietnamese: xà phòng

Hmong: xu npus

Pilipino: sabon

Chinese: 肥皂

French: savon

soccer ball (SAHK-ur bahl)

Spanish: bola de fútbol

Vietnamese: banh túc cầu

Hmong: npas ncaws, pob ncaws

Pilipino: saker

Chinese: 足球

French: ballon de football

sock (sahk)

Spanish: calcetín

Vietnamese: bi thất ngắn

Hmong: tham khwm

Pilipino: medyas

Chinese: 袜子 / 襪子

French: chaussette

a
b
c
d
e
f
g
h
i
j
k
l
m
n
o
p
q
r
s
t
u
v
w
x
y
z

A
B
C
D
E
F
G
H
I
J
K
L
M
N
O
P
Q
R
S
T
U
V
W
X
Y
Z

soda (SOH-duh)

Spanish: soda

Vietnamese: sô đa

Hmong: dej qab zib

Pilipino: soda

Chinese: 汽水

French: boisson gazeuse

sofa (SOH-fuh)

Spanish: sofá

Vietnamese: ghế nệm dài

Hmong: roojzaum

Pilipino: supa

Chinese: 沙发椅／沙發椅

French: canapé

soldier (SOHL-jur)

Spanish: soldado

Vietnamese: người lính

Hmong: tub nrog

Pilipino: sundalo

Chinese: 军人／軍人

French: soldat

soup (soop)

Spanish: sopa

Vietnamese: canh

Hmong: kua zaub, kua nqaij

Pilipino: sabaw

Chinese: 汤／湯

French: potage

space capsule (spays KAP-sul)

Spanish: cápsula espacial

Vietnamese: khoang tàu vũ trụ

Hmong: space capsule

Pilipino: kapsulang pangkalawakan

Chinese: 太空舱／太空艙

French: capsule spatiale

space shuttle
(spays SHUT-ul)

Spanish: transbordador especial **Pilipino:** sasakyang pangkalawakan

Vietnamese: tàu con thoi **Chinese:** 太空船

Hmong: lub nyooj hoom mus saum ntuj **French:** navette spatiale

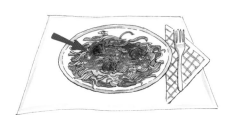

spaghetti (spuh-GET-ee)

Spanish: espagueti **Pilipino:** spagheti

Vietnamese: mì ống **Chinese:** 细通心面 / 細通心麵

Hmong: spaghetti **French:** spaghetti

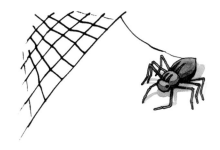

spider (SPY-dur)

Spanish: araña **Pilipino:** gagamba

Vietnamese: con nhện **Chinese:** 蜘蛛

Hmong: kab laug sab **French:** araignée

spinach (SPIN-ich)

Spanish: espinaca **Pilipino:** espinaka

Vietnamese: rau bó xôi **Chinese:** 菠菜

Hmong: ib hom zaub **French:** épinards

spoon (spoon)

Spanish: cuchara **Pilipino:** kutsara

Vietnamese: cái muỗng **Chinese:** 匙

Hmong: diav **French:** cuillère

spring (spring)

Spanish: primavera

Pilipino: tag-sibol

Vietnamese: mùa xuân

Chinese: 春

Hmong: ncaij nplooj ntoos hlav

French: printemps

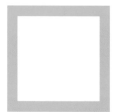

square (skwayr)

Spanish: cuadrado

Pilipino: parisukat

Vietnamese: hình vuông

Chinese: 正方

Hmong: plaub ces kaum ntev sib luag

French: carré

squirrel (skwurl)

Spanish: ardilla

Pilipino: ardilya

Vietnamese: con sóc

Chinese: 松鼠

Hmong: nas ncuav

French: écureuil

stairs (stayrz)

Spanish: escaleras

Pilipino: hagdan

Vietnamese: thang lầu

Chinese: 楼梯 / 樓梯

Hmong: ntaiv

French: escalier

star (star)

Spanish: estrella

Pilipino: bituin

Vietnamese: ngôi sao

Chinese: 星

Hmong: hnub qub

French: étoile

A B C D E F G H I J K L M N O P Q R *S* T U V W X Y Z

Sounds Like Fun!

What do you get when you take the *star* **out of** *starfish*? **What do you get when you take the** *berry* **out of** *strawberry*? **Now ask a friend these questions.**

starfish (STAR-fish)

Spanish: estrellamar
Vietnamese: con sao biển
Hmong: ntses hnub qub

Pilipino: isdang-bituin
Chinese: 海星
French: étoile de mer

station wagon (STAY-shun WAG-un)

Spanish: furgoneta familiar
Vietnamese: xe có chỗ để hành lý phí sau
Hmong: tsheb

Pilipino: station wagon
Chinese: 小厢型车 / 小厢型車
French: break

stomach (STUM-uk)

Spanish: estómago
Vietnamese: bao tử
Hmong: lub plab

Pilipino: tiyan
Chinese: 肚子
French: estomac

stove (stohv)

Spanish: estufa
Vietnamese: bếp lò
Hmong: qhov cub

Pilipino: kalan
Chinese: 炉子 / 爐子
French: fourneau, cuisinière

strawberry (STRAH-bayr-ee)

Spanish: fresa
Vietnamese: trái dâu
Hmong: strawberry

Pilipino: istroberi
Chinese: 草莓
French: fraise

a b c d e f g h i j k l m n o p q r *s* t u v w x y z

street (street)

Spanish: calle

Pilipino: daan

Vietnamese: đường phố

Chinese: 街道

Hmong: kev

French: rue

submarine (SUB-muh-reen)

Spanish: submarino

Pilipino: submarino

Vietnamese: tàu ngầm

Chinese: 潜水艇 / 潛水艇

Hmong: nkoj mus hauv qab thu dej

French: sous-marin

suit (soot)

Spanish: traje

Pilipino: terno

Vietnamese: bột đồ vét

Chinese: 西裝 / 西裝

Hmong: suit

French: costume

summer (SUM-ur)

Spanish: verano

Pilipino: tag-araw

Vietnamese: mùa hè

Chinese: 夏

Hmong: caij ntuj sov

French: été

Sunday (SUN-day)

Spanish: domingo

Pilipino: Linggo

Vietnamese: Chủ Nhật

Chinese: 星期日

Hmong: Sunday

French: dimanche

A
B
C
D
E
F
G
H
I
J
K
L
M
N
O
P
Q
R
S
T
U
V
W
X
Y
Z

sweater (SWET-ur)

Spanish: suéter

Pilipino: suweter

Vietnamese: áo len cổ chui

Chinese: 毛衣

Hmong: tsho tuaj plaub sov

French: pull-over

sweet potato
(sweet puh-TAY-toh)

Spanish: batata

Pilipino: kamote

Vietnamese: khoai lang

Chinese: 红薯 / 地瓜

Hmong: qos liab

French: patate douce

swing (swing)

Spanish: columpio

Pilipino: duyan

Vietnamese: cái đu

Chinese: 秋千 / 鞦韆

Hmong: viav vias

French: balançoire

a
b
c
d
e
f
g
h
i
j
k
l
m
n
o
p
q
r
s
t
u
v
w
x
y
z

A
B
C
D
E
F
G
H
I
J
K
L
M
N
O
P
Q
R
S
T
U
V
W
X
Y
Z

table (TAY-bul)

Spanish: mesa   **Pilipino:** mesa

Vietnamese: cái bàn   **Chinese:** 桌子

Hmong: rooj   **French:** table

taco (TAH-coh)

Spanish: taco   **Pilipino:** tako

Vietnamese: bánh tráng kẹp thịt   **Chinese:** 墨西哥食物

Hmong: taco   **French:** taco

tape player (tayp PLAY-ur)

Spanish: tocacintas, grabadora   **Pilipino:** tugtugan ng teyp

Vietnamese: máy hát băng   **Chinese:** 录音机／錄放音機

Hmong: lub thev   **French:** lecteur de cassettes

teacher (TEE-chur)

Spanish: profesor, maestro   **Pilipino:** guro

Vietnamese: thầy giáo   **Chinese:** 教师／教師

Hmong: kws qhia ntawv, xib fwb, nai ku   **French:** professeur

teapot (TEE-paht)

Spanish: tetera   **Pilipino:** tsarera

Vietnamese: bình trà   **Chinese:** 茶壶／茶壺

Hmong: hwj kais   **French:** théière

telephone
(TEL-uh-fohn)

Spanish: teléfono

Pilipino: telepono

Vietnamese: điện thoại

Chinese: 电话 / 電話

Hmong: xov tooj

French: téléphone

television
(TEL-uh-vih-zhun)

Spanish: televisión, televisor

Pilipino: telebisyon

Vietnamese: máy truyền hình

Chinese: 电视[机] / 電視機

Hmong: t.v.

French: télévision

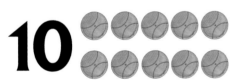

10

ten balls

ten (ten)

Spanish: diez

Pilipino: sampu

Vietnamese: mười

Chinese: 十

Hmong: kaum

French: dix

tenth (tenth)

Spanish: décimo

Pilipino: pansampu

Vietnamese: thứ mười

Chinese: 第十

Hmong: thib kaum

French: dixième

third (thurd)

Spanish: tercero

Pilipino: pangatlo

Vietnamese: thứ ba

Chinese: 第三

Hmong: ntib peb

French: troisième

Dictionary Detective

Find three food words that begin with the letter p. What are they?

thirteen (thur-TEEN)

13

thirteen erasers

Spanish: trece

Vietnamese: mười ba

Hmong: kaum peb

Pilipino: labing-tatlo

Chinese: 十三

French: treize

thirty (THUR-tee)

30

thirty dots

Spanish: treinta

Vietnamese: ba mươi

Hmong: peb caug

Pilipino: tatlumpu

Chinese: 三十

French: trente

three (three)

3

three chicks

Spanish: tres

Vietnamese: ba

Hmong: peb

Pilipino: tatlo

Chinese: 三

French: trois

thumb (thum)

Spanish: pulgar

Vietnamese: ngón tay cái

Hmong: ntiv tes xoo

Pilipino: hinlalaki

Chinese: 拇指

French: pouce

Thursday (THURZ-day)

Spanish: jueves

Vietnamese: Thứ Năm

Hmong: Thursday

Pilipino: Huwebes

Chinese: 星期四

French: jeudi

tiger (TY-gur)

Spanish: tigre

Pilipino: tigre

Vietnamese: con cọp

Chinese: 虎

Hmong: tsov

French: tigre

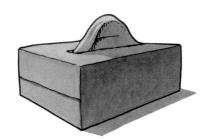

tissue (TISH-oo)

Spanish: pañuelo de papel

Pilipino: tisyu

Vietnamese: giấy lau mềm

Chinese: 纸巾／紙巾

Hmong: ntaub so ntswg

French: mouchoir en papier

toast (tohst)

Spanish: pan tostado

Pilipino: brindis

Vietnamese: bánh mì nướng

Chinese: 吐司面包／吐司麵包

Hmong: toast

French: toast

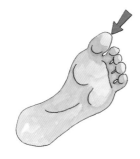

toe (toh)

Spanish: dedo del pie

Pilipino: daliri sa paa

Vietnamese: ngón chân

Chinese: 脚趾／腳指

Hmong: ntiv taw xoo,
ntiv taw thawj

French: orteil

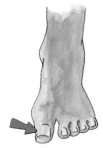

toenail (TOH-nayl)

Spanish: uña del dedo del pie

Pilipino: kuko sa paa

Vietnamese: móng chân

Chinese: 脚趾甲／腳指甲

Hmong: rau taw

French: ongle d'orteil

a
b
c
d
e
f
g
h
i
j
k
l
m
n
o
p
q
r
s
t
u
v
w
x
y
z

A
B
C
D
E
F
G
H
I
J
K
L
M
N
O
P
Q
R
S
T
U
V
W
X
Y
Z

toilet (TOY-lit)

Spanish: inodoro, lavabo   **Pilipino:** banyo

Vietnamese: nhà vệ sinh   **Chinese:** 马桶 / 馬桶

Hmong: chaw zaum tawm rooj, qhov viv   **French:** toilette

tomato (tuh-MAY-toh)

Spanish: tomate   **Pilipino:** kamatis

Vietnamese: cà chua   **Chinese:** 蕃茄

Hmong: txiv lws liab, txiv lws suav   **French:** tomate

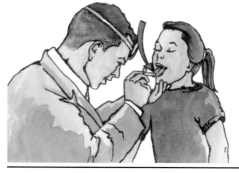

tongue (tung)

Spanish: lengua   **Pilipino:** dila

Vietnamese: cái lưỡi   **Chinese:** 舌

Hmong: plaig   **French:** langue

tools

tool (tool)

Spanish: herramienta   **Pilipino:** kasangkapan

Vietnamese: dụng cụ   **Chinese:** 工具

Hmong: ciaj   **French:** outil

tooth (tooth)

Spanish: diente   **Pilipino:** ngipin

Vietnamese: cái răng   **Chinese:** 牙齿 / 牙齒

Hmong: kaus hniav   **French:** dent

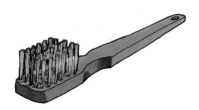

toothbrush
(TOOTH-brush)

Spanish: cepillo de dientes   **Pilipino:** sepilyo sa ngipin

Vietnamese: bàn chải răng   **Chinese:** 牙刷

Hmong: tus txhuam hniav   **French:** brosse à dents

toothpaste
(TOOTH-payst)

Spanish: pasta dental   **Pilipino:** kremang pansipilyo

Vietnamese: kem đánh răng   **Chinese:** 牙膏

Hmong: tshuaj txhuam hniav   **French:** dentifrice

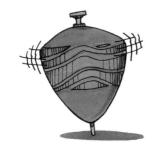

top (tahp)

Spanish: trompo   **Pilipino:** turompo

Vietnamese: con vụ   **Chinese:** 陀螺

Hmong: tu lub   **French:** toupie

tow truck (toh truk)

Spanish: carro de remolque, grúa   **Pilipino:** trak pang hatak

Vietnamese: xe dùng để kéo xe khác   **Chinese:** 拖车／拖吊車

Hmong: tsheb cab   **French:** dépanneuse

towel (TOU-ul)

Spanish: toalla   **Pilipino:** tuwalya

Vietnamese: khăn tắm, khăn lau   **Chinese:** 毛巾

Hmong: phuam   **French:** serviette

a b c d e f g h i j k l m n o p q r s t u v w x y z

A B C D E F G H I J K L M N O P Q R S **T** U V W X Y Z

trailer (TRAY-lur)

Spanish: remolque   **Pilipino:** treyler

Vietnamese: toa móc   **Chinese:** 拖车／拖曳車

Hmong: lub laub cab tom qab   **French:** remorque

train (trayn)

Spanish: tren   **Pilipino:** tren

Vietnamese: xe lửa   **Chinese:** 火车／火車

Hmong: tsheb ciav hlau   **French:** train

trash can (trash kan)

Spanish: cesto de la basura   **Pilipino:** basura

Vietnamese: thùng đựng rác   **Chinese:** 垃圾筒

Hmong: thoob khib nyiab   **French:** poubelle

trash collector
(trash kuh-LEK-tur)

Spanish: colector de la basura   **Pilipino:** basurero

Vietnamese: xe lấy rác   **Chinese:** 清洁工／清潔隊員

Hmong: tus neeg thauj khib nyiab   **French:** éboueur

tree (tree)

Spanish: árbol   **Pilipino:** puno

Vietnamese: cây   **Chinese:** 树木／樹木

Hmong: ntoo   **French:** arbre

triangle (TRY-ayng-gul)

Spanish: triángulo   **Pilipino:** tatsulok

Vietnamese: hình tam giác   **Chinese:** 三角形

Hmong: peb ceg   **French:** triangle

tricycle (TRY-sik-ul)

Spanish: triciclo   **Pilipino:** trisiklo, traysikel

Vietnamese: xe đạp ba bánh   **Chinese:** 三轮脚踏车／三輪車

Hmong: luv thim peb lub log   **French:** tricycle

truck (truk)

Spanish: camioneta, camión   **Pilipino:** trak

Vietnamese: xe tải   **Chinese:** 卡车／卡車

Hmong: truck   **French:** camionnette, camion

truck driver (truk DRY-vur)

Spanish: camionero   **Pilipino:** tsuper ng trak

Vietnamese: tài xế xe tải   **Chinese:** 卡车驾驶员／卡車駕駛員

Hmong: tus neeg tshav (truck)   **French:** conducteur de camion

Tuesday (TOOZ-day)

Spanish: martes   **Pilipino:** Martes

Vietnamese: Thứ Ba   **Chinese:** 星期二

Hmong: Tuesday   **French:** mardi

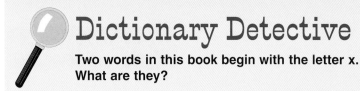

Dictionary Detective

Two words in this book begin with the letter x.
What are they?

A B C D E F G H I J K L M N O P Q R S **T** U V W X Y Z

turkey (TUR-kee)

Spanish: pavo   **Pilipino:** pabo

Vietnamese: gà tây   **Chinese:** 火鸡 / 火雞

Hmong: qaib ntxhw   **French:** dinde

turtle (TUR-tul)

Spanish: tortuga   **Pilipino:** pagong

Vietnamese: con rùa   **Chinese:** 乌龟 / 烏龜

Hmong: vaub kib   **French:** tortue

---

twelve (twelv)

12
twelve pencils

Spanish: doce   **Pilipino:** labindalawa

Vietnamese: mười hai   **Chinese:** 十二

Hmong: kaum ob   **French:** douze

---

twenty (TWEN-tee)

20
twenty dots

Spanish: veinte   **Pilipino:** dalawampu

Vietnamese: hai mươi   **Chinese:** 二十

Hmong: nees nkaum   **French:** vingt

---

two (too)

2

two cupcakes

Spanish: dos   **Pilipino:** dalawa

Vietnamese: hai   **Chinese:** 二

Hmong: ob   **French:** deux

---

typewriter (TYP-ryt-ur)

Spanish: máquina de escribir

Vietnamese: máy đánh chữ

Hmong: tshuab ntaus ntawv

Pilipino: makinilya

Chinese: 打字机／打字機

French: machine à écrire

Uu Uu

umbrella (um-BREL-uh)

Spanish: paraguas   **Pilipino:** payong

Vietnamese: cây dù   **Chinese:** 伞 / 傘

Hmong: lub kaus   **French:** parapluie

uncle (UN-kul)

Spanish: tío   **Pilipino:** tiyo

Vietnamese: cậu, chú, bác   **Chinese:** 伯父,叔父,姑父,姨丈/
                                伯父,叔父,姑丈,姨丈

Hmong: dab laug, txiv hlob, **French:** oncle
txiv ntxawm

underwear
(UN-dur-wayr)

Spanish: ropa interior   **Pilipino:** pangilalim

Vietnamese: đồ lót   **Chinese:** 内衣裤 / 內衣褲

Hmong: ris tshos xuab   **French:** sous-vêtements

vacuum cleaner
(VAK-yoom KLEEN-ur)

Spanish: aspiradora

Vietnamese: máy hút bụi

Hmong: cav qus tsev

Pilipino: bakyum

Chinese: 吸尘器 / 吸塵器

French: aspirateur

van (van)

Spanish: furgoneta, camioneta

Vietnamese: xe van

Hmong: lub vees

Pilipino: ban

Chinese: 行理车 / 行李車

French: camionnette

VCR (vee-see-AR)

Spanish: VCR

Vietnamese: máy chiếu video

Hmong: lub VCR

Pilipino: VCR

Chinese: 录像机 / 錄影機

French: magnétoscope

veterinarian
(vet-ur-uh-NAYR-ee-un)

Spanish: veterinario

Vietnamese: bác sĩ thú y

Hmong: kws kho tsiaj mob

Pilipino: beterinaryo

Chinese: 兽医 / 獸醫

French: vétérinaire

videotape
(VID-ee-oh-tayp)

Spanish: videocinta, cinta magnética para grabar

Vietnamese: băng video

Hmong: ka xev

Pilipino: vidiyo

Chinese: 录像带 / 錄影帶

French: vidéocassette

a
b
c
d
e
f
g
h
i
j
k
l
m
n
o
p
q
r
s
t
u
v
w
x
y
z

wagon (WA-gun)

Spanish: vagoneta

Pilipino: karo

Vietnamese: toa xe

Chinese: 小拖车 / 小拖車

Hmong: lub laub

French: charrette

waist (wayst)

Spanish: cintura

Pilipino: baywang

Vietnamese: eo, chỗ thắt lưng

Chinese: 腰部

Hmong: duav

French: taille

waiter (WAY-tur)

Spanish: camarero, mesero

Pilipino: serbidor

Vietnamese: người hầu bàn

Chinese: 侍者

Hmong: tus txiv neej nqa zaub tom lab no mov

French: serveur

waitress (WAY-tris)

Spanish: camarera, mesera

Pilipino: serbidora

Vietnamese: nữ hầu bàn

Chinese: 女侍

Hmong: tus poj niam nqa zaub tom lab noj mov

French: serveuse

washcloth (WAHSH-kloth)

Spanish: toallita para lavarse

Pilipino: bimpo

Vietnamese: khăn lau mặt

Chinese: 毛巾

Hmong: phuam ntxuav muag

French: gant de toilette

washing machine
(WAHSH-ing muh-SHEEN)

Spanish: lavadora

Vietnamese: máy giặt

Hmong: tshuab ntxhua khaub ncaws

Pilipino: makinang pang laba

Chinese: 洗衣机 / 洗衣機

French: machine à laver

wastebasket
(WAYST-bas-kit)

Spanish: cesto de los papeles

Vietnamese: sọt rác

Hmong: thoob khib nyiab

Pilipino: basurahang basket

Chinese: 废纸篓 / 廢紙簍

French: corbeille à papier

watch (wahch)

Spanish: reloj

Vietnamese: cái đồng hồ

Hmong: moos

Pilipino: relos

Chinese: 手表 / 手錶

French: montre

water (WAH-tur)

Spanish: agua

Vietnamese: nước

Hmong: dej

Pilipino: tubig

Chinese: 水

French: eau

watermelon
(WAH-tur-mel-un)

Spanish: sandía

Vietnamese: trái dưa hấu

Hmong: dib liab

Pilipino: pakwan

Chinese: 西瓜

French: pastèque

a b c d e f g h i j k l m n o p q r s t u v **w** x y z

web site (web syt)

Spanish: sitio web, página de Internet

Vietnamese: trang mạng

Hmong: web site

Pilipino: web site

Chinese: 网站 / 網站

French: site web

Wednesday (WENZ-day)

Spanish: miércoles

Vietnamese: Thứ Tư

Hmong: Wednesday

Pilipino: Miyerkules

Chinese: 星期三

French: mercredi

whale (wayl)

Spanish: ballena

Vietnamese: con cá voi

Hmong: ib hom ntses loj

Pilipino: balyena

Chinese: 鲸鱼 / 鯨魚

French: baleine

wheel (weel)

Spanish: rueda, llanta

Vietnamese: bánh xe

Hmong: thob log

Pilipino: gulong

Chinese: 轮 / 輪

French: roue

whistle (WIS-ul)

Spanish: silbato, pito

Vietnamese: cái còi

Hmong: lub pib tshuab

Pilipino: silbato

Chinese: 口哨 / 口哨

French: siffler

A
B
C
D
E
F
G
H
I
J
K
L
M
N
O
P
Q
R
S
T
U
V
W
X
Y
Z

Dictionary Detective

White is a color. Find the word in this book that is a color which ends in the letter w. What is it?

white (wyt)

Spanish: blanco   **Pilipino:** puti

Vietnamese: màu trắng   **Chinese:** 白色

Hmong: dawb   **French:** blanc

window (WIN-doh)

Spanish: ventana   **Pilipino:** bintana

Vietnamese: cửa sổ   **Chinese:** 窗

Hmong: qhov rai   **French:** fenêtre

winter (WIN-tur)

Spanish: invierno   **Pilipino:** taglamig

Vietnamese: mùa đông   **Chinese:** 冬

Hmong: caij ntuj no   **French:** hiver

wolf (woolf)

Spanish: lobo   **Pilipino:** lobo

Vietnamese: chó sói   **Chinese:** 狼

Hmong: ob qus   **French:** loup

woman (WUM-un)

Spanish: mujer   **Pilipino:** babae

Vietnamese: người đàn bà **Chinese:** 女子

Hmong: poj niam   **French:** femme

a b c d e f g h i j k l m n o p q r s t u v **w** x y z

131

worm (wurm)

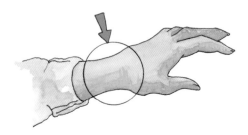

Spanish: gusano

Vietnamese: con sâu

Hmong: cua nab

Pilipino: bulati

Chinese: 虫 / 蟲

French: ver

wrist (rist)

Spanish: muñeca

Vietnamese: cổ tay

Hmong: dab teg

Pilipino: pupulsuhan

Chinese: 手腕

French: poignet

x-ray (EKS-ray)

Spanish: radiografía   **Pilipino:** eks ray

Vietnamese: tia x   **Chinese:** X射线 / X光線

Hmong: xoo fai fab   **French:** rayon X

xylophone
(ZY-luh-fohn)

Spanish: xilófono   **Pilipino:** saylopon

Vietnamese: đàn gõ   **Chinese:** 木琴

Hmong: xylophone   **French:** xylophone

a
b
c
d
e
f
g
h
i
j
k
l
m
n
o
p
q
r
s
t
u
v
w
x
y
z

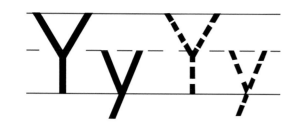

yam (yam)

Spanish: ñame

Vietnamese: khoai từ,
khoai mỡ

Hmong: qos liab

Pilipino: tugi

Chinese: 红薯 / 地瓜

French: patate douce

yard (yard)

Spanish: patio

Vietnamese: cái sân

Hmong: tog tsev

Pilipino: bakuran

Chinese: 庭院

French: cour

yarn (yarn)

Spanish: hilado

Vietnamese: sợi chỉ

Hmong: paws ntuag, xov paj

Pilipino: sinulid

Chinese: 纱 / 紗

French: laine

yellow (YEL-oh)

Spanish: amarillo

Vietnamese: màu vàng

Hmong: daj

Pilipino: dilaw

Chinese: 黄色

French: jaune

zebra (ZEE-bruh)

Spanish: cebra

Vietnamese: con ngựa vằn

Hmong: nees txaij

Pilipino: sebra

Chinese: 斑马 / 斑馬

French: zèbre

zipper (ZIP-ur)

Spanish: cremallera, cierre

Vietnamese: khóa kéo

Hmong: txoj swb

Pilipino: siper

Chinese: 拉链 / 拉鍊

French: fermeture éclair

zoo (zoo)

Spanish: parque zoológico

Vietnamese: sở thú

Hmong: chaw yug tsiaj hav zoov

Pilipino: soolohiko

Chinese: 动物园 / 動物園

French: zoo

---

zucchini (zoo-KEE-nee)

Spanish: calabacín

Vietnamese: bí xanh nhỏ

Hmong: taub ntev

Pilipino: kalabasa

Chinese: 意大利南瓜 / 意大利瓜

French: courgette

a
b
c
d
e
f
g
h
i
j
k
l
m
n
o
p
q
r
s
t
u
v
w
x
y
z

NUMBERS

Numbers 1-20

1   2   3   4   5

6   7   8   9   10

11   12   13   14   15

16   17   18   19   20

Numbers by Tens to 100

10   60

20   70

30   80

40   90

50   100

Ordinal Numbers

tenth

ninth
eighth
seventh

sixth

fifth
fourth

third

second

first

COLORS

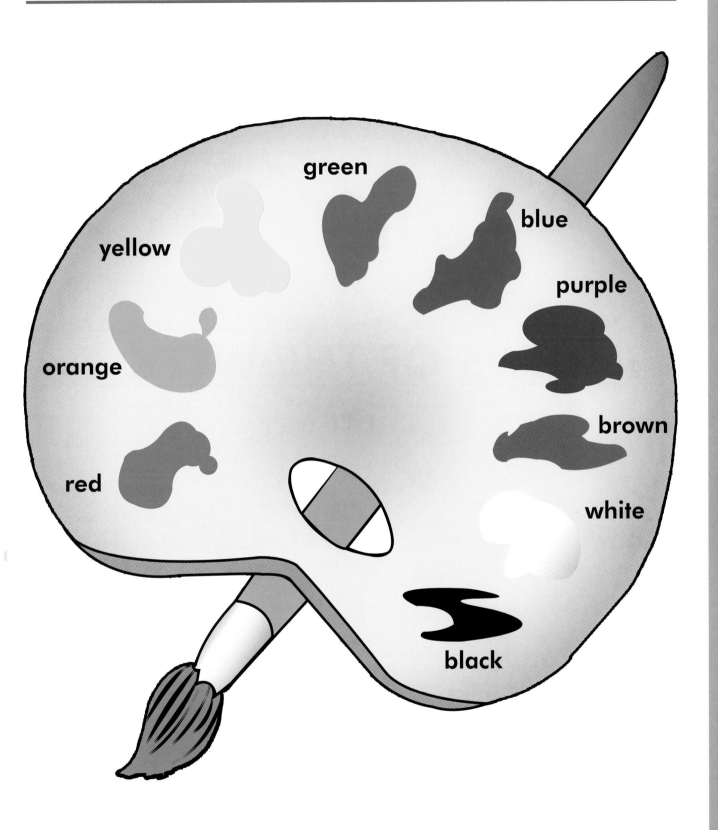

green

blue

yellow

purple

orange

brown

red

white

black

MONTHS OF THE YEAR

January

Sunday	Monday	Tuesday	Wednesday	Thursday	Friday	Saturday
	1	2	3	4	5	6
7	8	9	10	11	12	13
14	15	16	17	18	19	20
21	22	23	24	25	26	27
28	29	30	31			

February

Sunday	Monday	Tuesday	Wednesday	Thursday	Friday	Saturday
				1	2	3
4	5	6	7	8	9	10
11	12	13	14	15	16	17
18	19	20	21	22	23	24
25	26	27	28			

March

Sunday	Monday	Tuesday	Wednesday	Thursday	Friday	Saturday
				1	2	3
4	5	6	7	8	9	10
11	12	13	14	15	16	17
18	19	20	21	22	23	24
25	26	27	28	29	30	31

April

Sunday	Monday	Tuesday	Wednesday	Thursday	Friday	Saturday
1	2	3	4	5	6	7
8	9	10	11	12	13	14
15	16	17	18	19	20	21
22	23	24	25	26	27	28
29	30					

May

Sunday	Monday	Tuesday	Wednesday	Thursday	Friday	Saturday
		1	2	3	4	5
6	7	8	9	10	11	12
13	14	15	16	17	18	19
20	21	22	23	24	25	26
27	28	29	30	31		

June

Sunday	Monday	Tuesday	Wednesday	Thursday	Friday	Saturday
					1	2
3	4	5	6	7	8	9
10	11	12	13	14	15	16
17	18	19	20	21	22	23
24	25	26	27	28	29	30

July

Sunday	Monday	Tuesday	Wednesday	Thursday	Friday	Saturday
1	2	3	4	5	6	7
8	9	10	11	12	13	14
15	16	17	18	19	20	21
22	23	24	25	26	27	28
29	30	31				

August

Sunday	Monday	Tuesday	Wednesday	Thursday	Friday	Saturday
			1	2	3	4
5	6	7	8	9	10	11
12	13	14	15	16	17	18
19	20	21	22	23	24	25
26	27	28	29	30	31	

September

Sunday	Monday	Tuesday	Wednesday	Thursday	Friday	Saturday
						1
2	3	4	5	6	7	8
9	10	11	12	13	14	15
16	17	18	19	20	21	22
23	24	25	26	27	28	29
30						

October

Sunday	Monday	Tuesday	Wednesday	Thursday	Friday	Saturday
	1	2	3	4	5	6
7	8	9	10	11	12	13
14	15	16	17	18	19	20
21	22	23	24	25	26	27
28	29	30	31			

November

Sunday	Monday	Tuesday	Wednesday	Thursday	Friday	Saturday
				1	2	3
4	5	6	7	8	9	10
11	12	13	14	15	16	17
18	19	20	21	22	23	24
25	26	27	28	29	30	

December

Sunday	Monday	Tuesday	Wednesday	Thursday	Friday	Saturday
1	2	3	4	5	6	7
8	9	10	11	12	13	14
15	16	17	18	19	20	21
22	23	24	25	26	27	28
29	30	31				

DAYS OF THE WEEK

January

Days of the Week →

Sunday	Monday	Tuesday	Wednesday	Thursday	Friday	Saturday
	1	2	3	4	5	6
7	8	9	10	11	12	13
14	15	16	17	18	19	20
21	22	23	24	25	26	27
28	29	30	31			

A Note to Teachers and Parents

Learning new words can be challenging for students, but give them a picture that illustrates the word and the task becomes much easier. Colorful illustrations capture the interest and imagination of students, making them more engaged in learning. The *IDEA Picture Dictionary* introduces students to basic vocabulary and gives them a foundation of dictionary and word attack skills. By developing these key skills, students will experience greater success as they learn to read.

The *IDEA Picture Dictionary* is easy to use. Entries are organized alphabetically, with letters down the side of each page and large letters marking the start of each section. Each entry includes a picture, English pronunciation*, and translations of the word into six languages. Throughout the dictionary you will find "✎Sounds Like Fun" activities to build students' understanding of sounds and "✐Dictionary Detective" activities to put their dictionary skills to work.

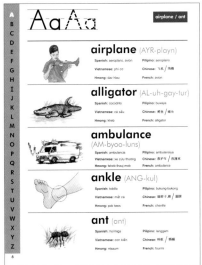

Using the *IDEA Picture Dictionary*

The *IDEA Picture Dictionary* can be used on its own or in conjunction with any English language development program, including *Carousel of IDEAS* and *IDEAS for Literature*.

To help students learn how to use the dictionary, read the introduction on pages 4 and 5 with them. Point out the main elements of the dictionary and discuss how to find information. Then read some of the "✐Dictionary Detective" activities and have students complete the challenge. For specific ideas on how to build phonics and language skills, read "Phonics Helps Build Reading Skills!" beginning on page 140. Also visit the web site noted below for wonderful activity sheets that you can download.

Internet Link to Language Development Activities

Please visit **www.ballard-tighe.com/picturedictionary.htm** for links to activities you can use with the *IDEA Picture Dictionary*. You will find fun activities that build vocabulary and phonics skills for elementary students as well as older students learning to read English.

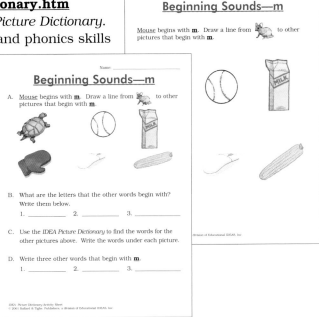

▶ *Activities are provided at two levels so you can choose the ones appropriate for your students.*

---

*Pronunciations are derived from the following three sources: *American Heritage College Dictionary, Third Edition*, 1997; *Oxford American Dictionary: Heald Colleges Edition*, 1986; and *Webster's New World College Dictionary, Fourth Edition*, 1999.

Phonics Helps Build Reading Skills!

Phonics is the process of attaching sounds (known as phonemes) to the letter or letters (graphemes) that represent those sounds. For example, if we know how to attach the /c/ /a/ /t/ sounds to the corresponding letters, we will be able to pronounce the printed word *cat*. By learning sound/symbol correspondences, students can pronounce words that may be unfamiliar to them. However, before students can make this connection between sounds and symbols, they must develop an understanding that language is made up of sounds that can be manipulated. This is called "phonemic awareness." Phonemic awareness is fundamental to reading. Read below how to help students build phonemic awareness and phonics skills. The 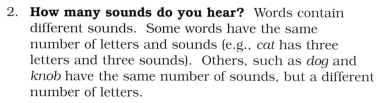 icon indicates suggested activities to build each skill.

THE FIRST BUILDING BLOCKS—SOUNDS

The following activities will help students develop an understanding of sounds in language (i.e., phonemic awareness):

1. **What sounds do you hear in *cat*?** It is important for students to identify the sounds in spoken words (e.g., cat = /c/ /a/ /t/).

   Say words very slowly and ask students to listen for each sound. Emphasize a specific sound that you want students to focus on, such as /t/ in *bat*. Point out words familiar to students that have the same phonic element, such as *hat* and *cat*. As students begin to master this skill, you can extend the activity by giving students *IDEA Picture* cards of words such as *hat*, *cat*, *flag*, and *desk* and asking them to find all the words that end with the same sound.

▲ *Have students find the words that end with the same sound.*

2. **How many sounds do you hear?** Words contain different sounds. Some words have the same number of letters and sounds (e.g., *cat* has three letters and three sounds). Others, such as *dog* and *knob* have the same number of sounds, but a different number of letters.

   Give students practice "hearing" the sounds of words by having them clap as they hear the sounds in words. Then have students create personal dictionaries of words that contain one, two, or three (or more) sounds.

3. **What difference does a sound make?** One sound can mean the difference between *hit* and *it*! It is important for students to know that a sound or several sounds in a word can be deleted to create new words.

   Play "Do As I Say" with sounds. Give prompts such as "Do as I say; take the /b/ away from *bat*. Do as I say; take the /h/ away from *hand*."

▲ *Have students create personal dictionaries, such as the one above made with a pattern from* Carousel of IDEAS.

4. **Can you make a new word by changing sounds?** We can make entirely new words by deleting sounds, as previously noted, as well as by substituting sounds. For example, *rag* becomes *tag* when we substitute /t/ for /r/.

⚒ Assign each student a sound, then pick a word such as *cake*. Point out the picture of cake in the *IDEA Picture Dictionary*. Ask each student in turn to replace the first sound in the word with his or her assigned sound to see if it makes a real word. You also can emphasize how sounds can be manipulated by identifying objects through rhyming words. Show a word from the *IDEA Picture Dictionary* or one of the *IDEA Picture* cards (e.g., pencil). Then say, "This is a tencil, fencil, pencil." Ask students to choose the word from the series that is the name of the picture.

5. **What makes these words similar?** Students must be able to identify the similarities in words. For example, what do /pen/, /pat/, and /pig/ have in common? [They all start with the /p/ sound!]

⚒ Integrate alliteration into everyday tasks. For example, when doing oral work with students, ask someone to bring you "the **b**ig, **b**lue **b**owl." Or, before lining up for lunch, ask students to find objects in the room that begin with a certain sound; as each student responds, he or she moves to the line. You can use the *IDEA Picture Dictionary* to teach students how to incorporate alliteration in their own sentences. Ask them to go to a section in the dictionary, e.g., the "Ll" section, and create phrases and sentences that integrate alliteration. For example, "Lola loves lemon lollipops." Have a contest to see which student can use the most words in an alliterative way.

▲ "Bring me the **b**ig, **b**lue **b**owl."

6. **Can you hear this sound?** Isolating sounds enables students to identify specific elements such as the initial sounds of words.

⚒ Show students a word such as *cow* in the *IDEA Picture Dictionary* or show an *IDEA Picture* card of the word. Ask students to say the first sound (/c/) and then pause before they say the rest of the word. When students master this, ask them to follow the same procedure for the final sound and then the medial sound.

7. **Does the cat wear a hat?** Rhyming demonstrates students' ability to hear relationships among words of similar sounds.

⚒ Make poetry a part of every day. Read poems, create rhymes about everyday activities (e.g., Let's have a **look** at this pretty **book**.), or play a game of "I am thinking of a word that rhymes with ____" to emphasize the sameness of words. Show a picture(s) from the *IDEA Picture Dictionary* or an *IDEA Picture* card and ask students to create a rhyming sentence. Encourage students to create their own poetry, using the pronunciations in the *IDEA Picture Dictionary* to help them with sounds and the words to help them with correct spelling.

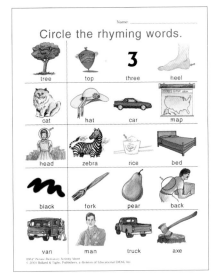

▲ *Rhyming activities are available at www.ballard-tighe.com/ picturedictionary.htm.*

8. **Do you want to play a /spl/endid game?** Phonemic blending allows students to put sounds together into a smoothly formed oral word.

⚒ Begin with small blending units, even with multisyllabic words. Show pictures of words such as *president, brown, dress,* and *sheep* in the *IDEA Picture Dictionary*. Ask students to sound out each word. Then ask them to attack more challenging words, e.g., *splendid.* Begin with /sp/, /spl/, /splen/, and continue until they have sounded out the entire word *splendid.* Students can create personal picture dictionaries or posters showing the splendid words they can pronounce.

ANOTHER BUILDING BLOCK—CONNECTING SOUNDS AND SYMBOLS

As soon as students understand that language is made up of sounds they can manipulate, they are ready to connect the sounds to symbols—and to read! Phonics skills help students attack unfamiliar written words. Students must master the four major phonics skills listed below.

1. **Recognize which letters or letter combinations represent sounds.** Students need to know which letters or combinations of letters represent particular sounds. For example, they must recognize that /t/ is the same sound at the beginning of the words *tap* and *tame* and that *ough* represents different sounds in *though* and *tough*. Since phonics adds the visual dimension to the sounds developed in phonemic awareness, it is time to emphasize the word in written form.

   1) Have students look at words in the *IDEA Picture Dictionary* that begin with the same letter. As they are looking at the written words, pronounce those words. This will emphasize the sound and the symbol that represents it. 2) Use word walls of words that have similar written elements but different pronunciations. Use these words in conversation and writing to solidify similarities and differences. 3) Create opportunities that give students continued exposure to words that have been presented orally. For example, give students various *IDEA Picture & Word* cards and ask them to put them into categories (e.g., according to beginning sounds or ending sounds). Students should be asked to use the words orally and in writing.

2. **Blending the individual sounds of a word together to form a true word.** Students must understand how to blend individual sounds to create words. For example, a student must be able to pronounce the individual sounds /f/ /i/ /sh/ and then to put those sounds together to make the word *fish*. For some learners, blending sounds is very difficult.

   1) Break words into smaller units or emphasize onset (initial letter or letters) and rhyme (remaining portion of the word). For example, ask students to say the beginning sound in the word *fish* (/f/). Then ask them what letter goes with the /f/ sound (f). Ask them to look up the word *fish* in the "Ff" section of the *IDEA Picture Dictionary*. Ask them to look at the word and pronounce the /f/ and then the /ish/ to produce *fish*. 2) Point out similar familiar words to build blending skills. For example, students who know the word *dish* will be better able to blend f-i-s-h.

   ▲ *Students must put the sounds /f/ /i/ /sh/ together to make the word* fish.

3. **Storing phonemes in their correct sequence.** Students must be able to produce sounds in the order in which the letters appear. Frequently students can attach sounds to individual letters one at a time, but are unable to then reproduce those sounds in the correct order. For example, a student may pronounce /r/ /i/ /p/ as individual sounds and then say the word as *pit* or *pear*.

   1) Have students use letter tiles to place the letters in sequence as they pronounce the sounds of a word. 2) Give students an *IDEA Word* card and allow them to move their fingers under the word so they point to each letter or letter combination. 3) Sometimes with emergent readers or those who have perceptual difficulties, it may be necessary to mark the first letter with a dot or color code it to stress its placement in the word. Remember that after students have sounded out the unfamiliar word, they need to say the word smoothly as a whole unit for it to become part of their vocabulary.

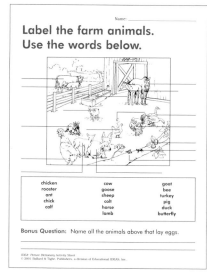

**Label the farm animals.
Use the words below.**

chicken	cow	goat
rooster	goose	bee
ant	sheep	turkey
chick	colt	pig
calf	horse	duck
	lamb	butterfly

Bonus Question: Name all the animals above that lay eggs.

IDEA Picture Dictionary Activity Sheet
© 2001 Ballard & Tighe, Publishers, a division of Educational IDEAS, Inc.

4. **Completing a memory search that matches phoneme combinations with real words that are part of their conceptual (meaning) vocabulary.** While phonics is often critical to word attack, comprehension is the ultimate objective of reading. Students may attach the correct sounds to the letters in a word such as *cove* but if they have no understanding of what a cove is, the reading act is not complete.

   1) Use the *IDEA Picture Dictionary* to point out the pictures of words. Seeing the word and picture emphasizes the connection between objects and printed words. 2) Use multisensory stimuli to be sure that words on the page are

   ▲ *Activities like this help students put new words in context. Download this activity sheet at* www.ballard-tighe.com/ picturedictionary.htm.

connected to ideas. Give students a chance to hear and see the word, trace it, write it in their notebook, and so forth. 3). Refer to the *IDEA Picture Dictionary* often to underscore its use as a reference tool and as a natural part of the students' learning strategy.

ⓉⒾⓅⓈ TO MAKE LANGUAGE DEVELOPMENT MORE EFFECTIVE AND FUN!

Dictionaries are excellent tools to reinforce the meaning of words. They are critical tools for students, especially those learning a new language. Here are severals tips to make language development—oral language as well as reading and writing—more effective and fun!

* **Provide as much oral language as possible.** Phonics is a sound-based system that needs oral reinforcement to be effective. In the classroom, students must have opportunities to hear and see the language in order to become proficient readers. Read stories, tell jokes, use audiotapes, have conversations, and ask open-ended questions. Encourage students to interview neighbors or classroom visitors, tell stories on the way to lunch, or point out objects while you describe them. Many, varied experiences with oral language are critical to reading success.

* **Encourage students to experiment with language.** Students who are just beginning the reading process and those who are having reading difficulties tend to apply the same sound whenever they see a letter. Encourage students to try various sounds and sound combinations until the word "sounds" like a real word to them. If they have difficulty using this "trial and error" approach, you may need to give them a "plan of attack" such as first use the short vowel sound, then try the long vowel, now try vowel combinations, and so forth. Emphasize that they have many strategies and tools to aid in their reading and writing, including this dictionary.

* **Use manipulatives.** The *IDEA Picture Dictionary*, *IDEA Picture & Word* cards, letter tiles, blocks, moveable letters, marking boards, erasers, and other manipulatives help students to develop phonics skills. Since the brain stores information in multiple places, it is critical to provide students with as much varied sensory input as possible to tap all areas of the brain. Encouraging students to see, hear, feel, and touch letters will enable them to tap various storage areas of the brain. A phonics skill such as exchanging one sound for another is a sophisticated activity. However, the task is much "simpler" when a letter is physically removed and another letter is put in its place using letter cards or other manipulatives.

* **Link to prior learning.** Students must attach new learning to prior knowledge. For example, if students already know how to read the word *cute*, they can relate that knowledge to attack an unfamiliar word such as *chute*. Remind students of the relationships between words they already know to ones that are unfamiliar to them. Making word walls or dictionaries of words that rhyme (e.g., cute, chute, brute) or contain similar phonic elements (e.g., lamb, comb, crumb) will encourage students to relate familiar words with new ones.

* **Apply phonics learning frequently in authentic settings.** Often, students can attack words in isolation (e.g., *cloak*), but have difficulty reading the word correctly in a sentence (e.g., The princess put her cloak around her shoulders.). Students must see the application of phonics in many settings (e.g., on word cards, on practice pages, in their readers) and practice them often in order for the sound/symbol relationships to become familiar. If students encounter the /ai/ combination often enough, they will recognize that combination when it appears in more complex words such as *remain*. Just because students have mastered the sound in the short term does not mean that the sound is permanently a part of their word attack repertoire. Students should see the new words in print (e.g., on word cards, on the board, in a sentence), hear the new words, and write the new words.

(continued)

* Introduce sounds in context. Introduce the sounds of the English language in context and provide examples of words that have those sounds. For example, /t/ is what we hear at the beginning of *toe*, *trumpet*, and *tiger*. Encourage students to make dictionaries, create word walls, use egg cartons to house pictures and/or words with similar elements, or make scrapbooks of pictures and words. This will help students understand how to apply the sounds. These activities also reinforce the connection between sounds and the letters that represent them.

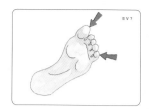

▲ *Readers need exposure to words in many settings such as word cards, practice pages, and readers.*

* Encourage students to write. Reading and writing are different sides of the same literacy coin. Students who write as they learn phonics tend to read faster and better than those who do not. This is especially true when students are encouraged to utilize personalized spelling for words that may not be part of their writing vocabulary. For example, writers who are willing to attempt to spell *tight* by producing *tite* or *tiet* are more likely to succeed in phonics than those who are reluctant to take such risks. Practice in producing the written form of words is an excellent way to both apply multisensory practice and demonstrate the relationship between sounds and the letters that represent them.

* Consider the students' native language. Students who are not native English speakers may encounter great difficulties with English. This is particularly true for students whose native language is not alphabetic (e.g., Chinese) or whose language is very phonetic (e.g., Spanish). Teachers need to focus on key phonics components and provide opportunities for English learners to practice seeing and hearing the sounds and letters. Moving too quickly from one new sound to another will confuse students and interfere with the mastery necessary to learn the elements. Provide visuals, such as *IDEA Picture & Word* cards, as well as actions to solidify a concept or word meaning and to make sure students hear and see the target words. You can help learners make the connections between ideas and words. Begin with pictures of simple, concrete words (e.g., *cat*, *house*, *tree*) and then move to more abstract ones (e.g., *government*, *helpers*, *structure*).

▲ *Give students many opportunities to write. The student work above comes from an IDEAS for Literature student journal.*